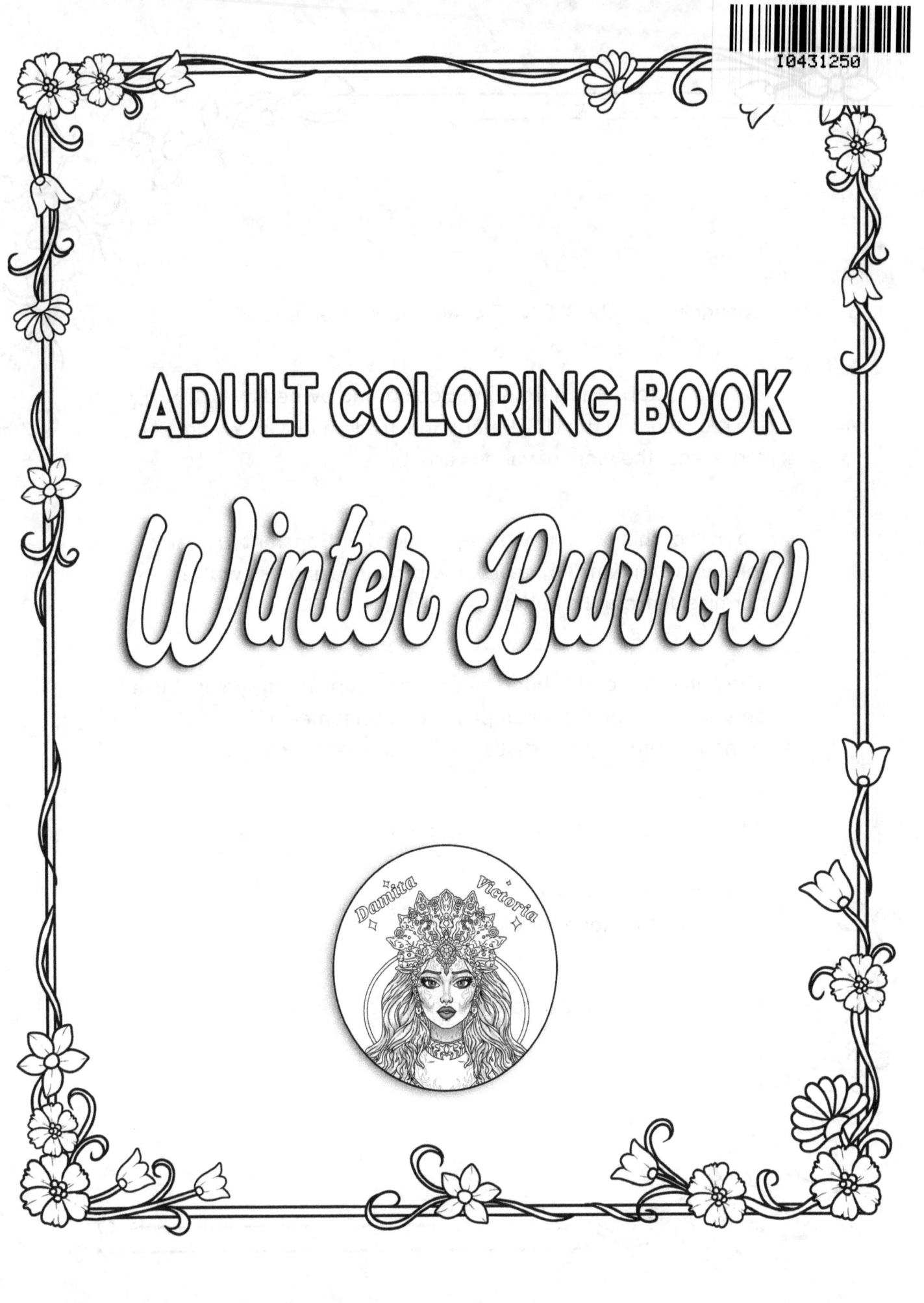

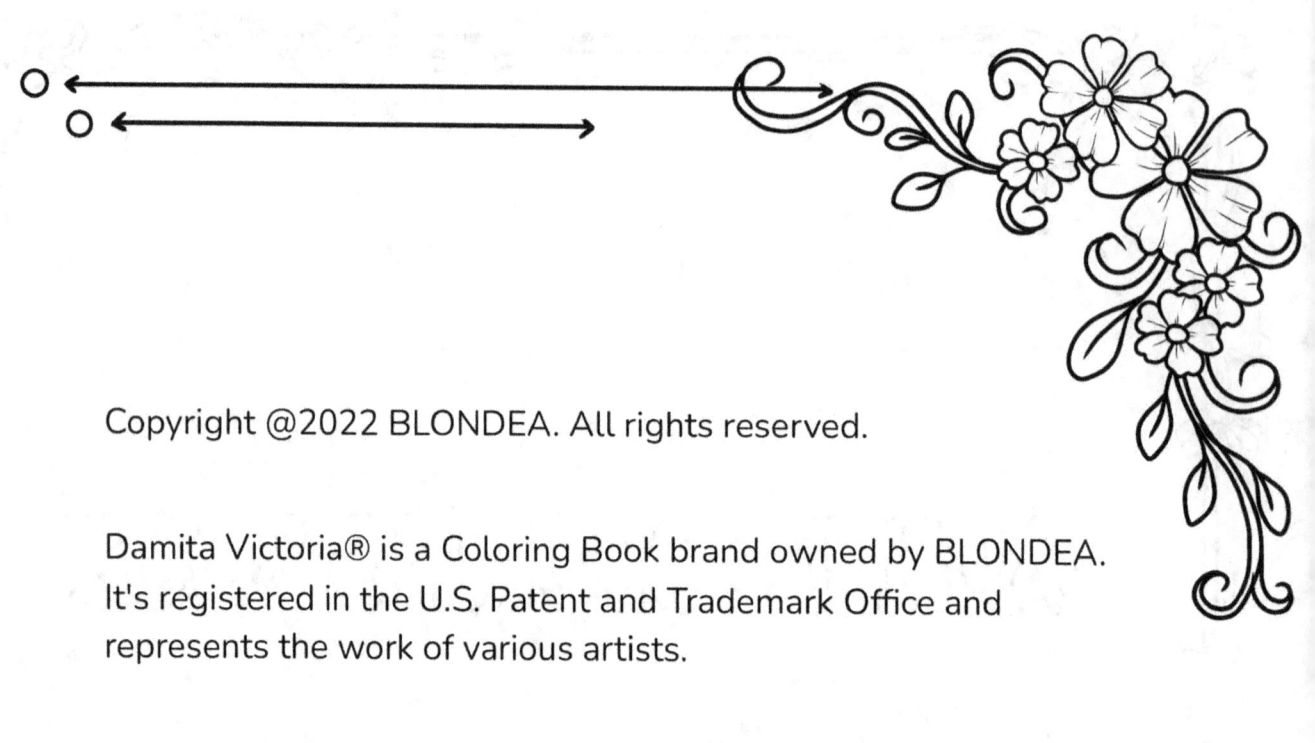

Copyright @2022 BLONDEA. All rights reserved.

Damita Victoria® is a Coloring Book brand owned by BLONDEA. It's registered in the U.S. Patent and Trademark Office and represents the work of various artists.

No part of this book may be reproduced or transmitted in any form or any means whatsoever without the express written permission from the author.

The purchaser of this book may scan or copy it for personal use only. You may post colored pages on social media if complemented by an artist's credit and the book's title.

If you have any questions or concerns, let us know at

hi@damitavictoria.com.
www.damitavictoria.com

Thank you for your support of the author's right.

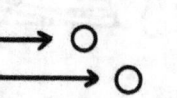

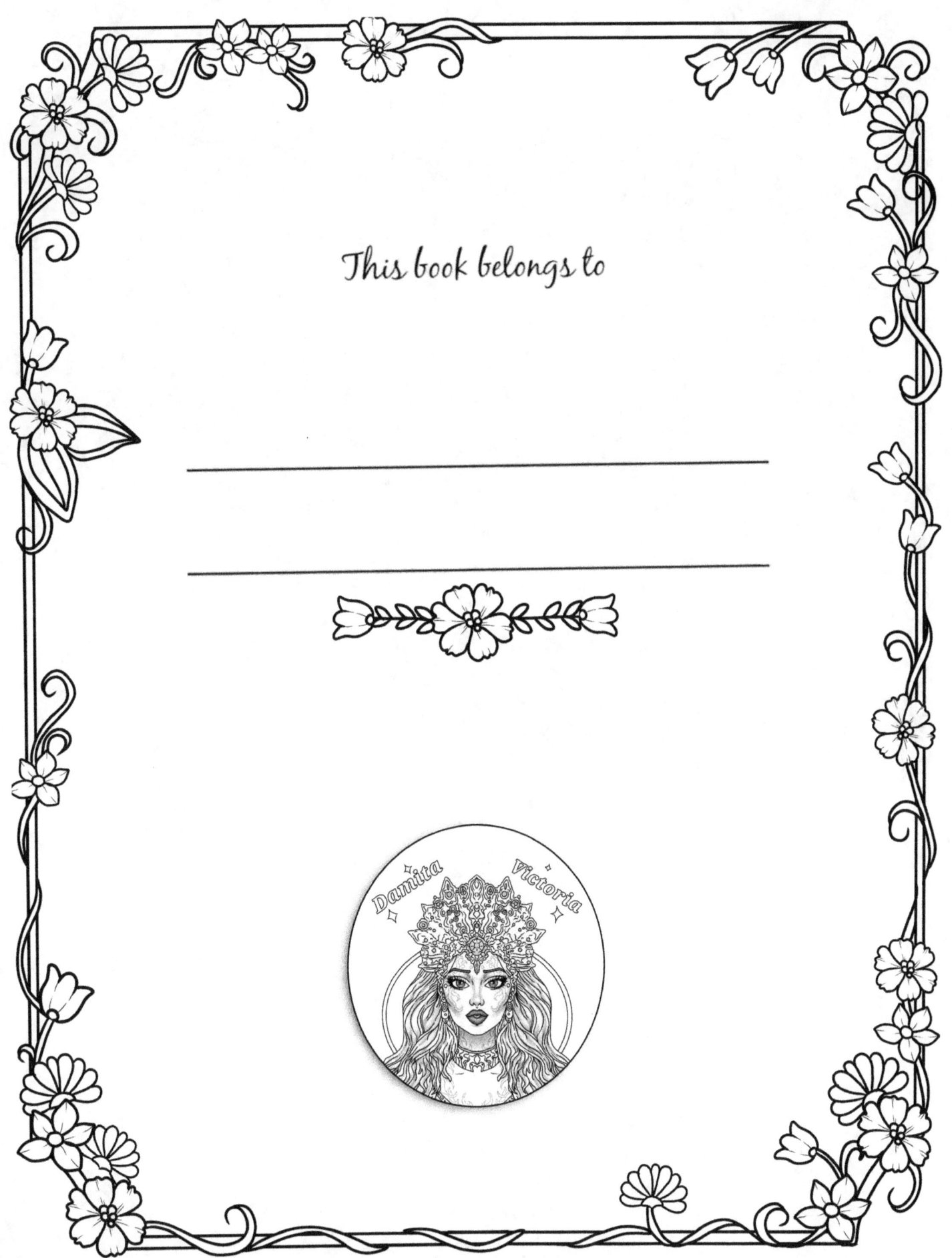

A Guide to Using This Book

- There are a total of 40 drawings in the book.

- Be sure to use soft-colored sharp pencils to get better results.

- Be careful of using other tools such as gel pens or markers. We recommend a piece of cardstock or thick paper behind the page you're working on to prevent the ink from bleeding to the page below.

- To find the best color combinations that match your needs, use a color test page to experiment with various tones. Be mindful, as colors occasionally might not match your expectations.

- Color whichever images you like, and skip whichever you don't feel inspired. You can come back the next day as we advised you to practice daily to get the most out of this experience.

- Share Your Creativity. Why keep that creativity hidden? We encourage you to share your colored pages with like-minded colorists like you. We would love to see your art masterpieces.

- It doesn't end here! Visit our website to unlock the hidden page and join our Facebook Group, Damita Victoria Artwork, to get more free images. How exciting!

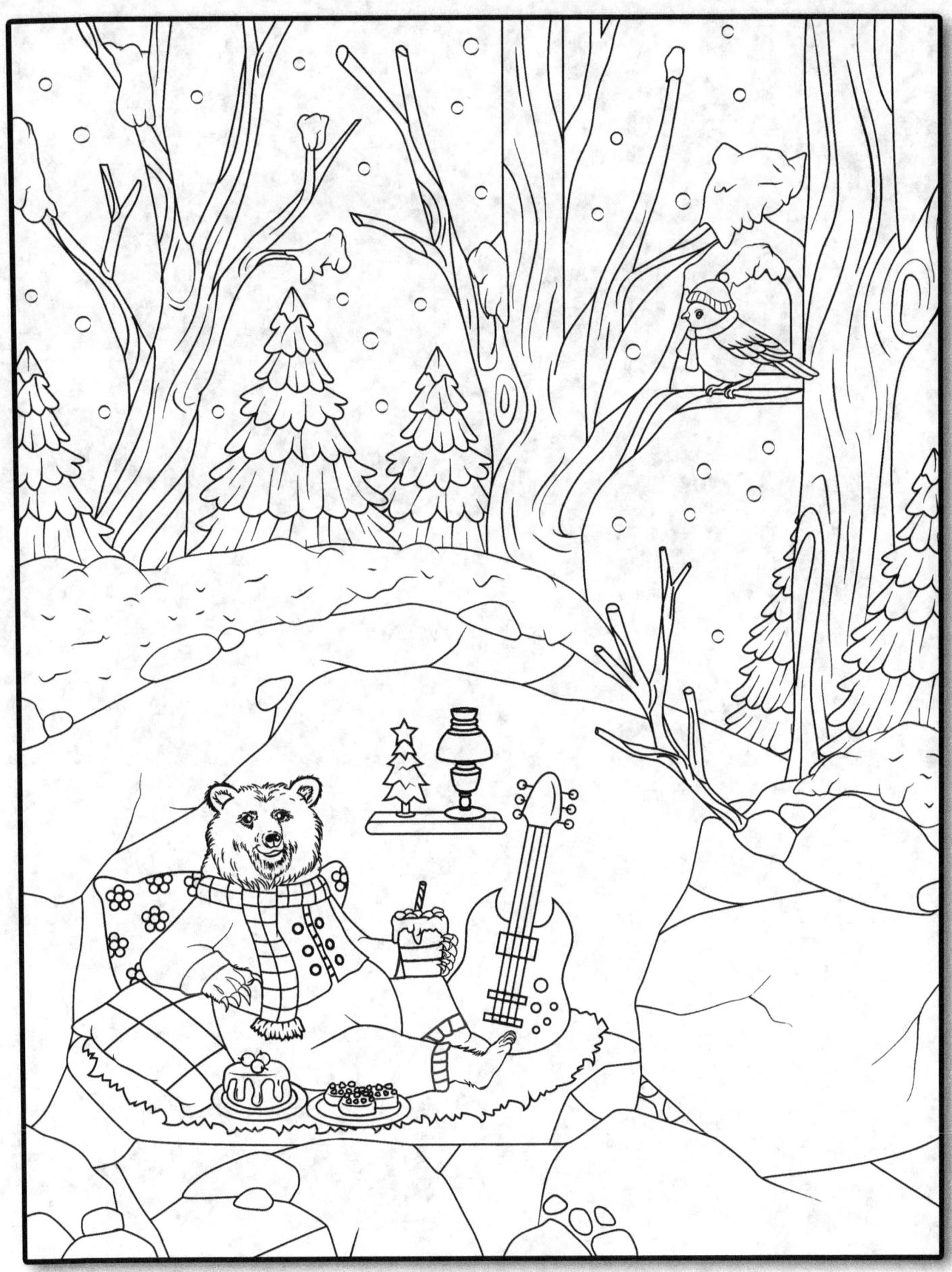

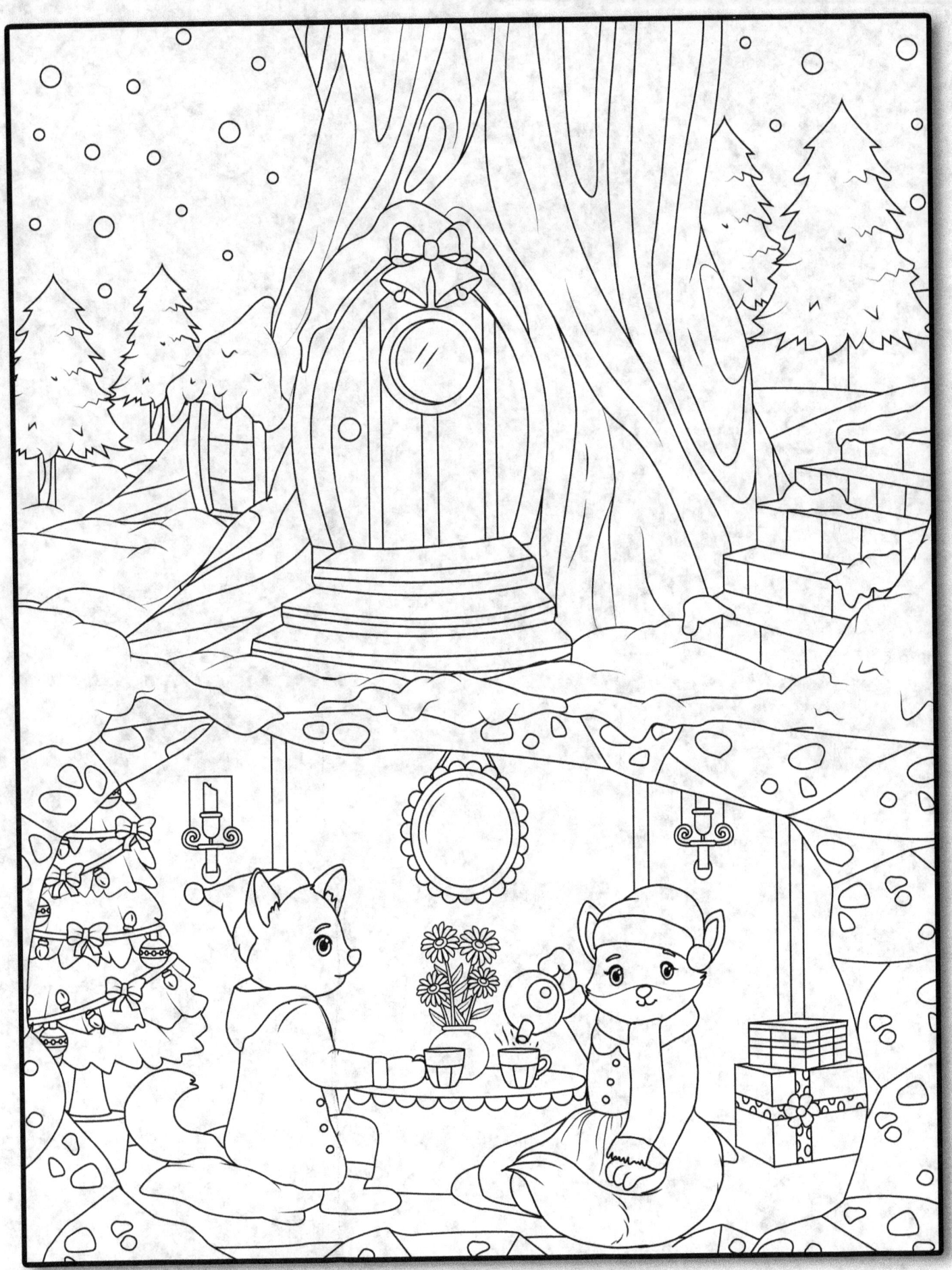

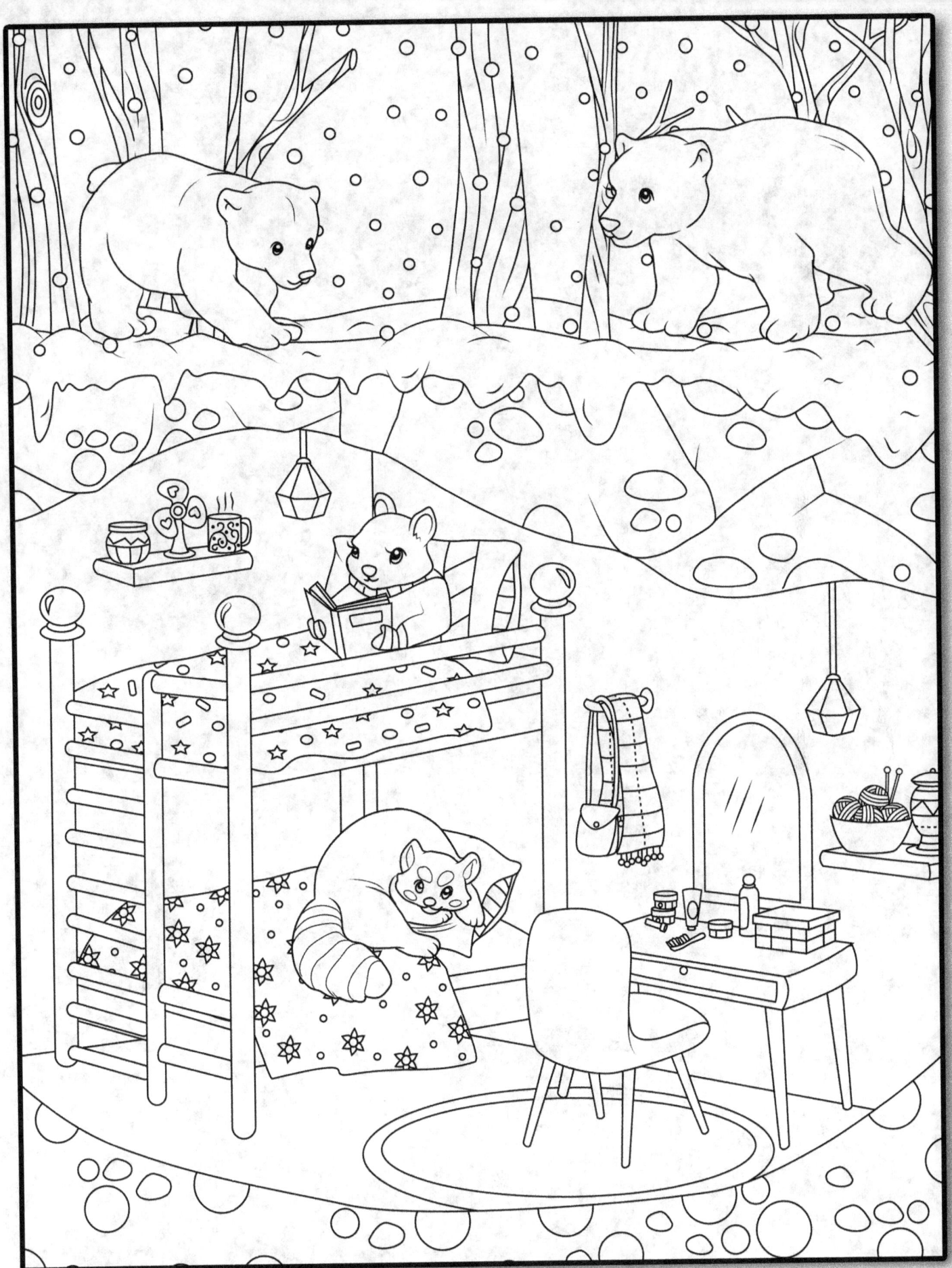

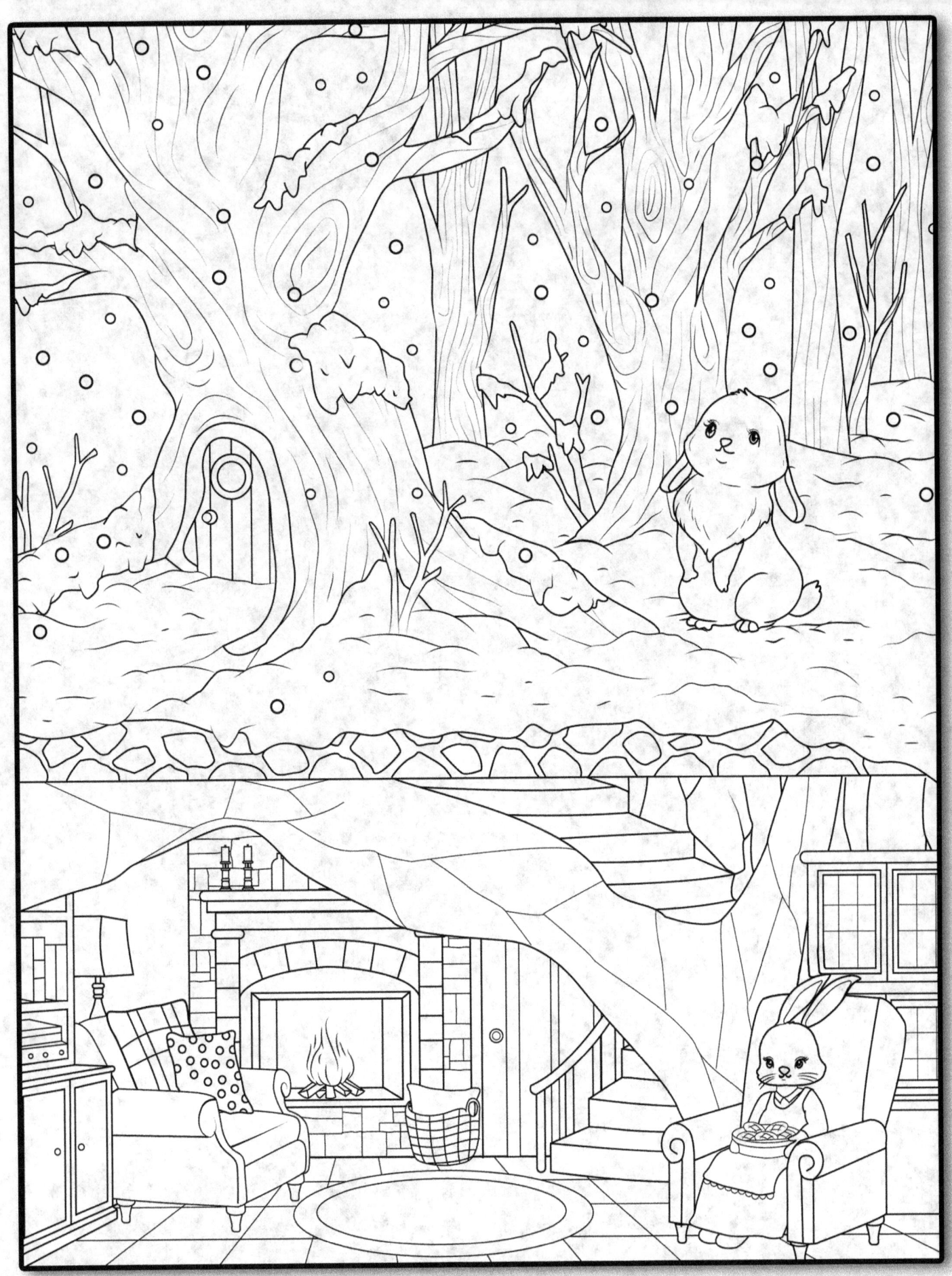

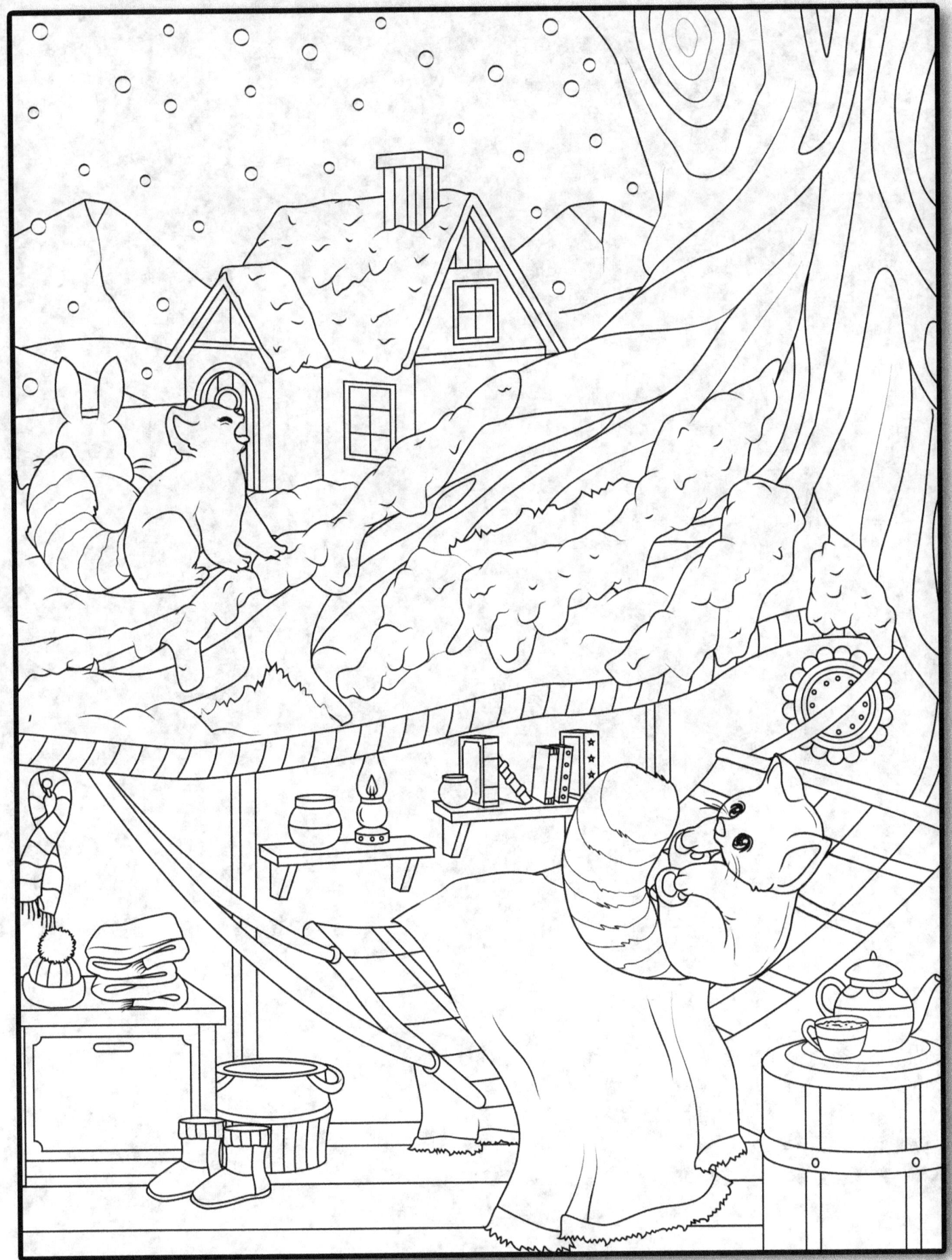

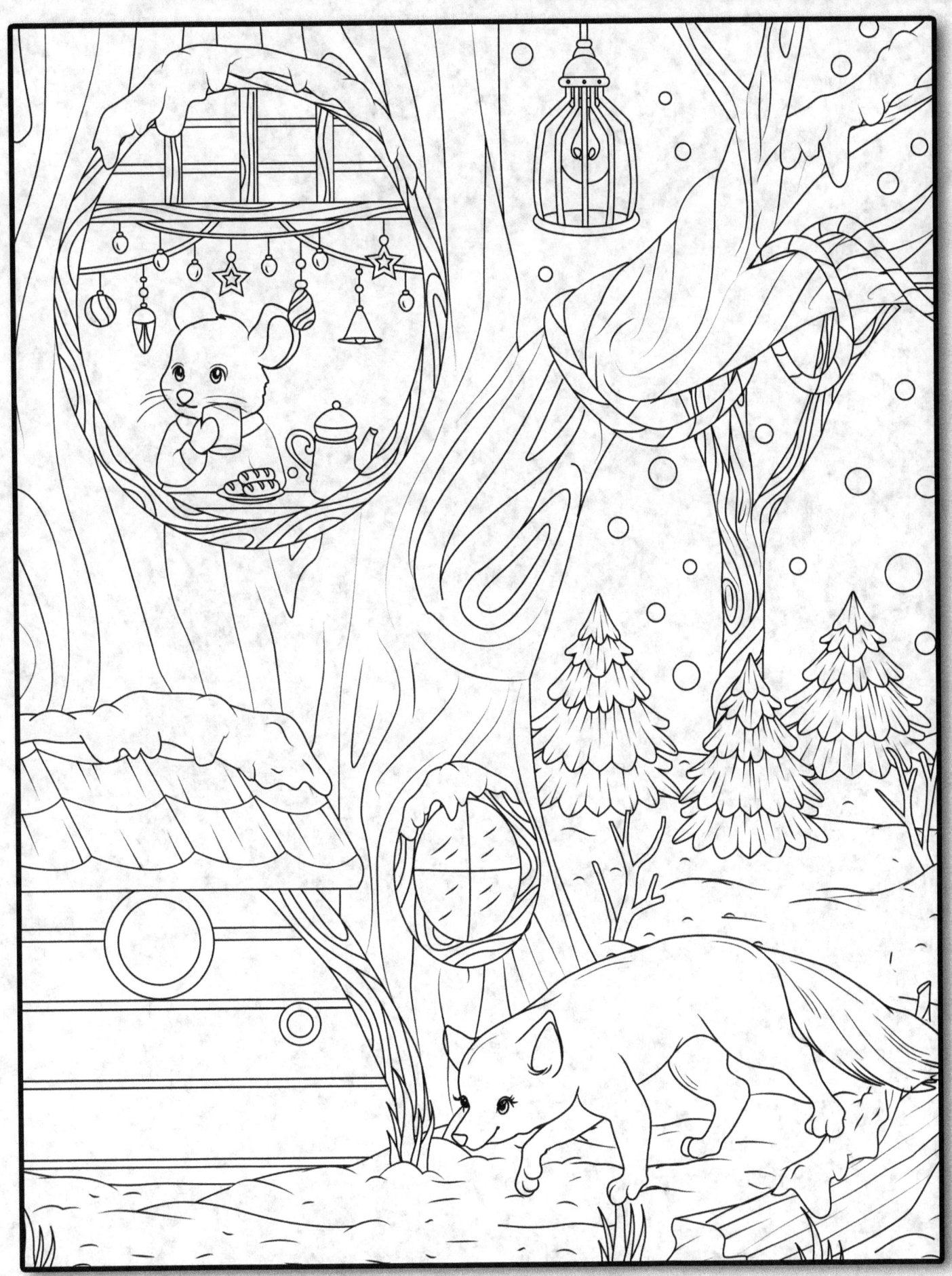

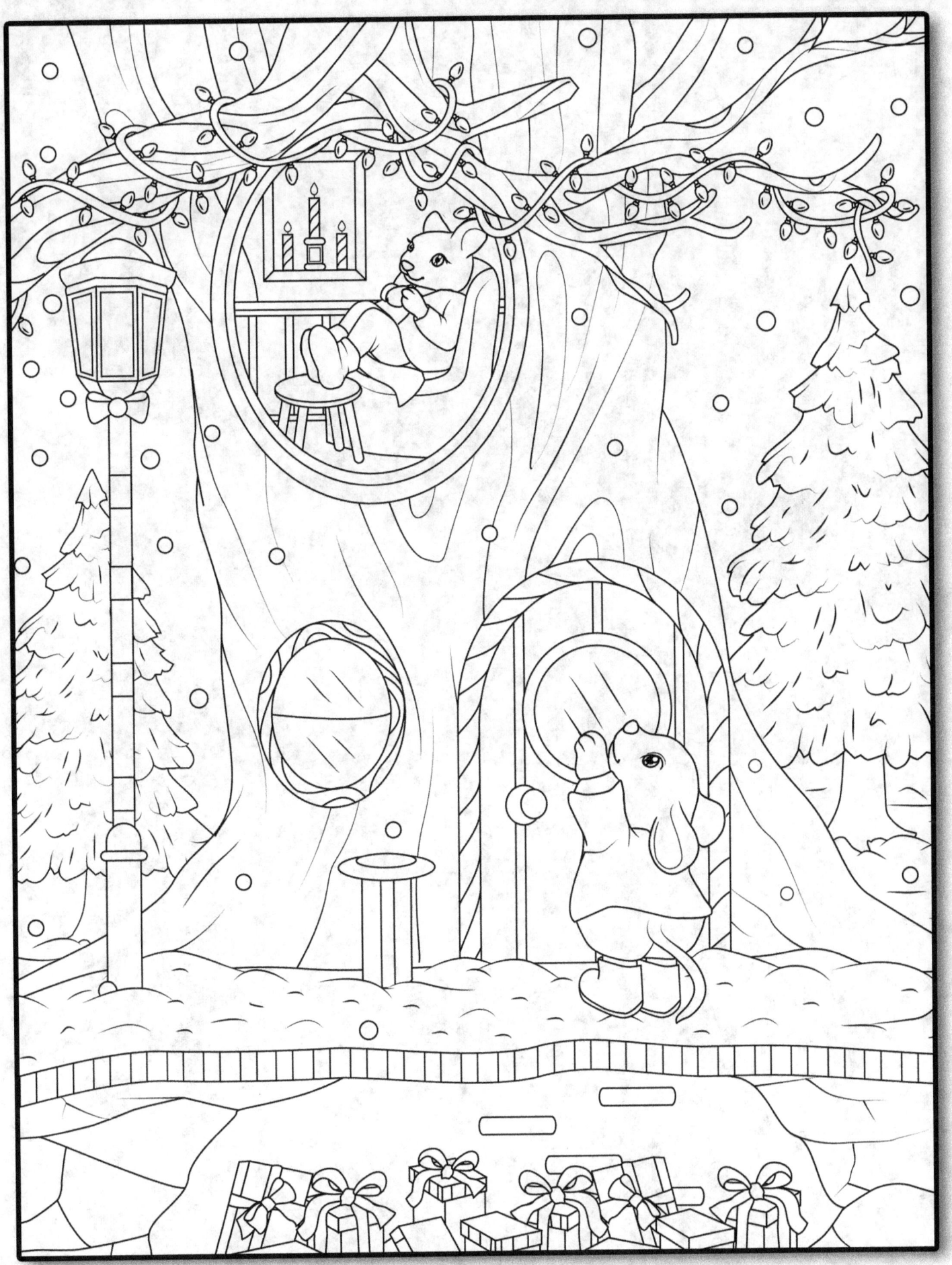

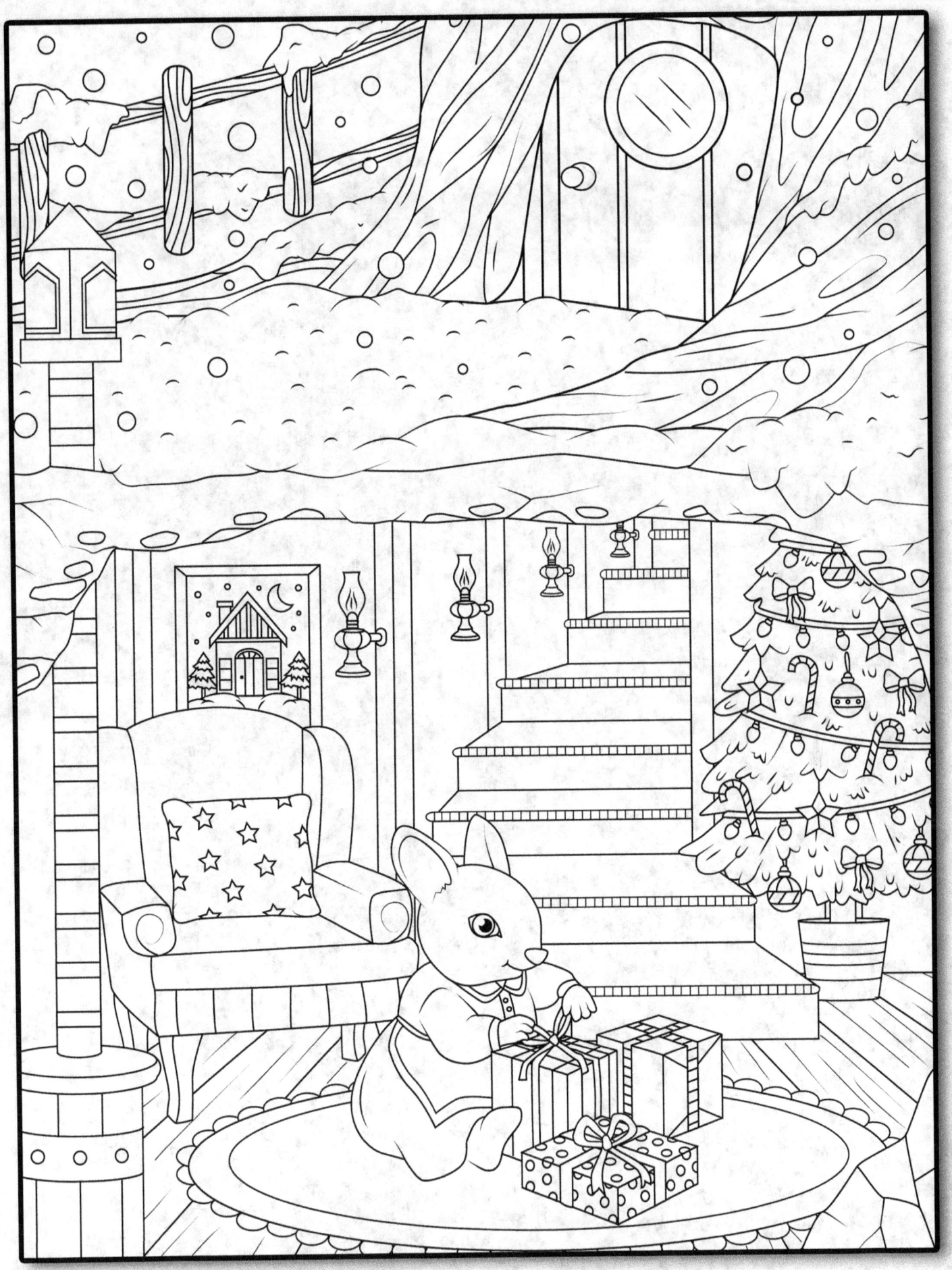

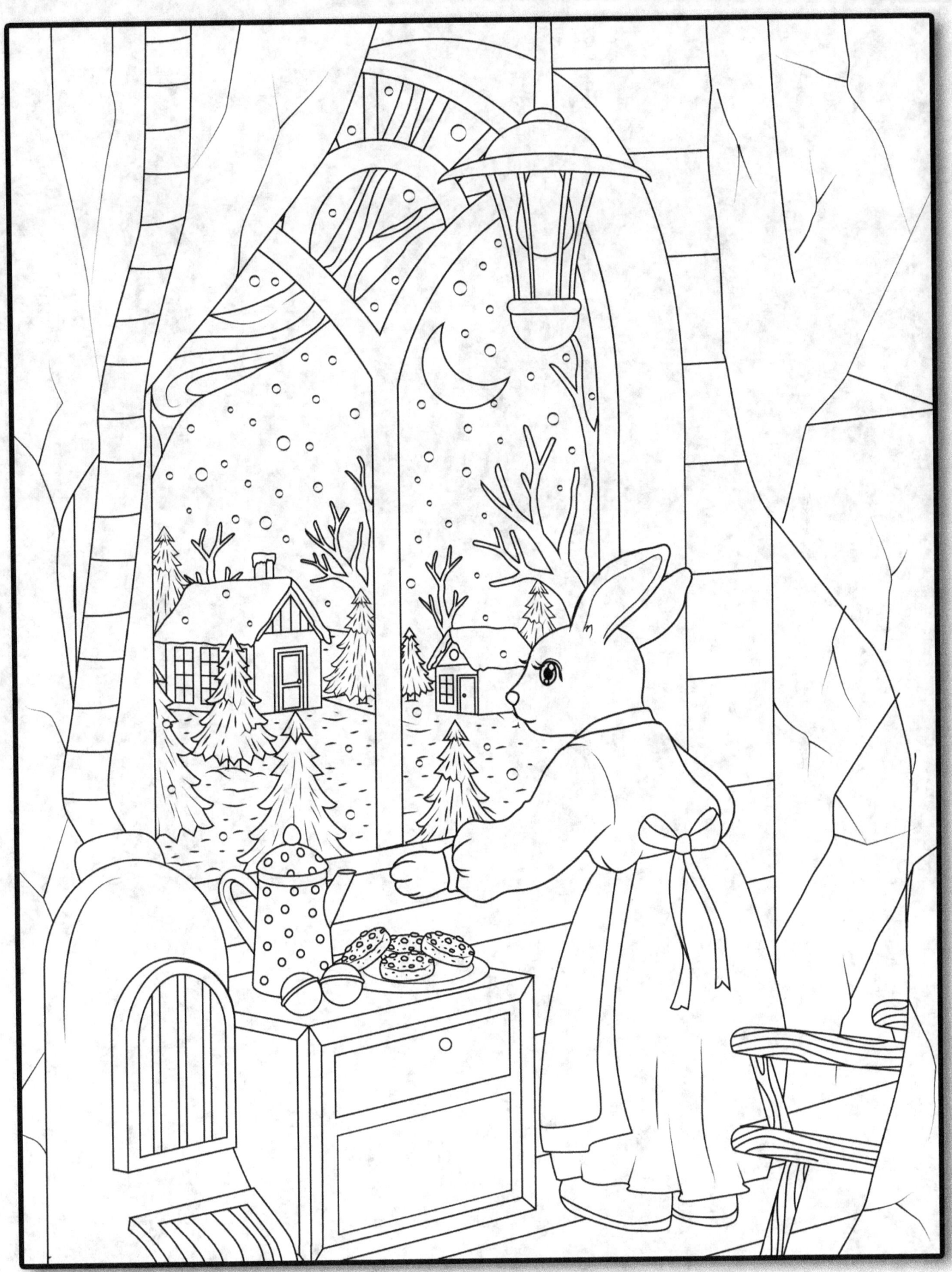

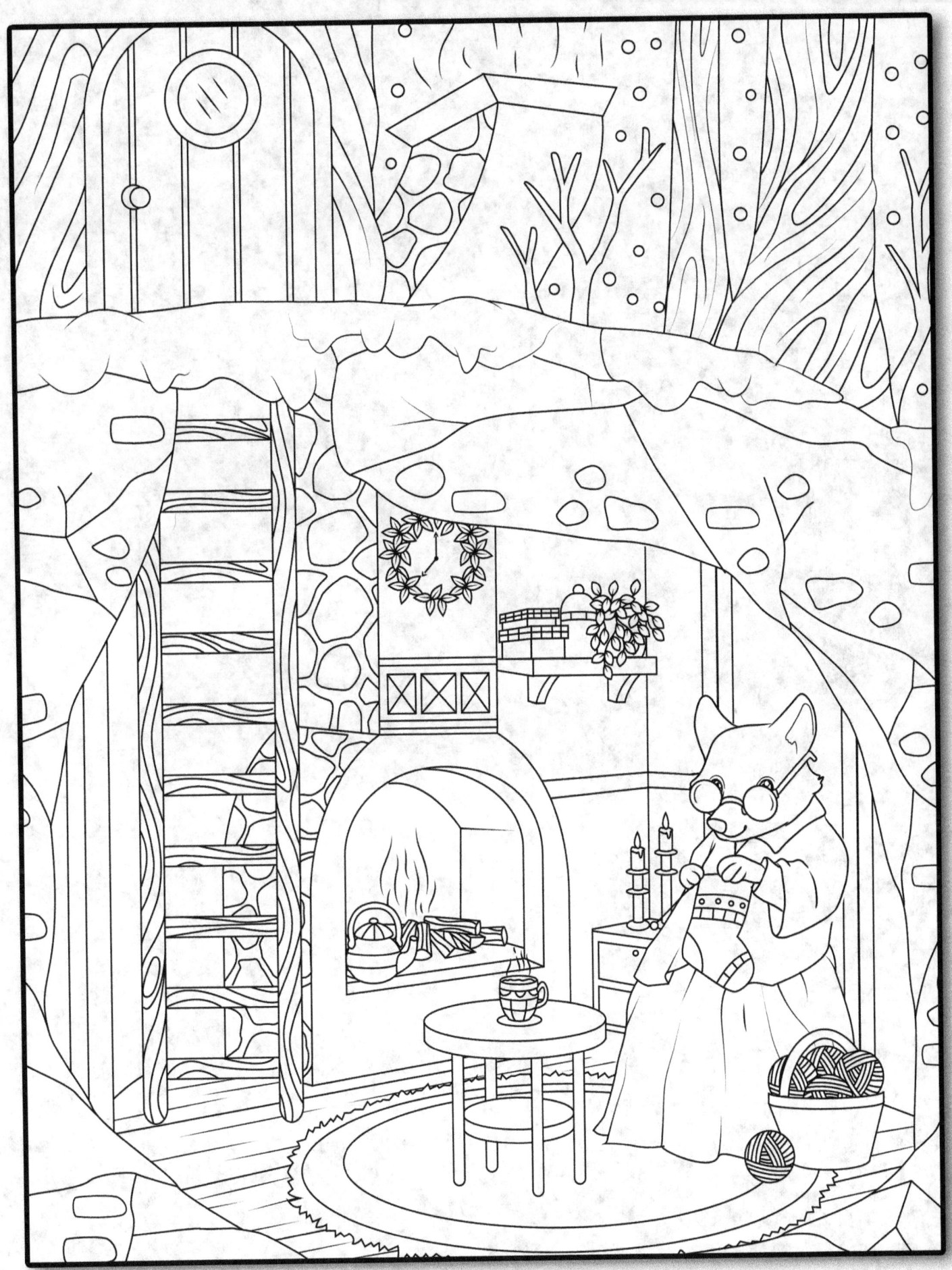

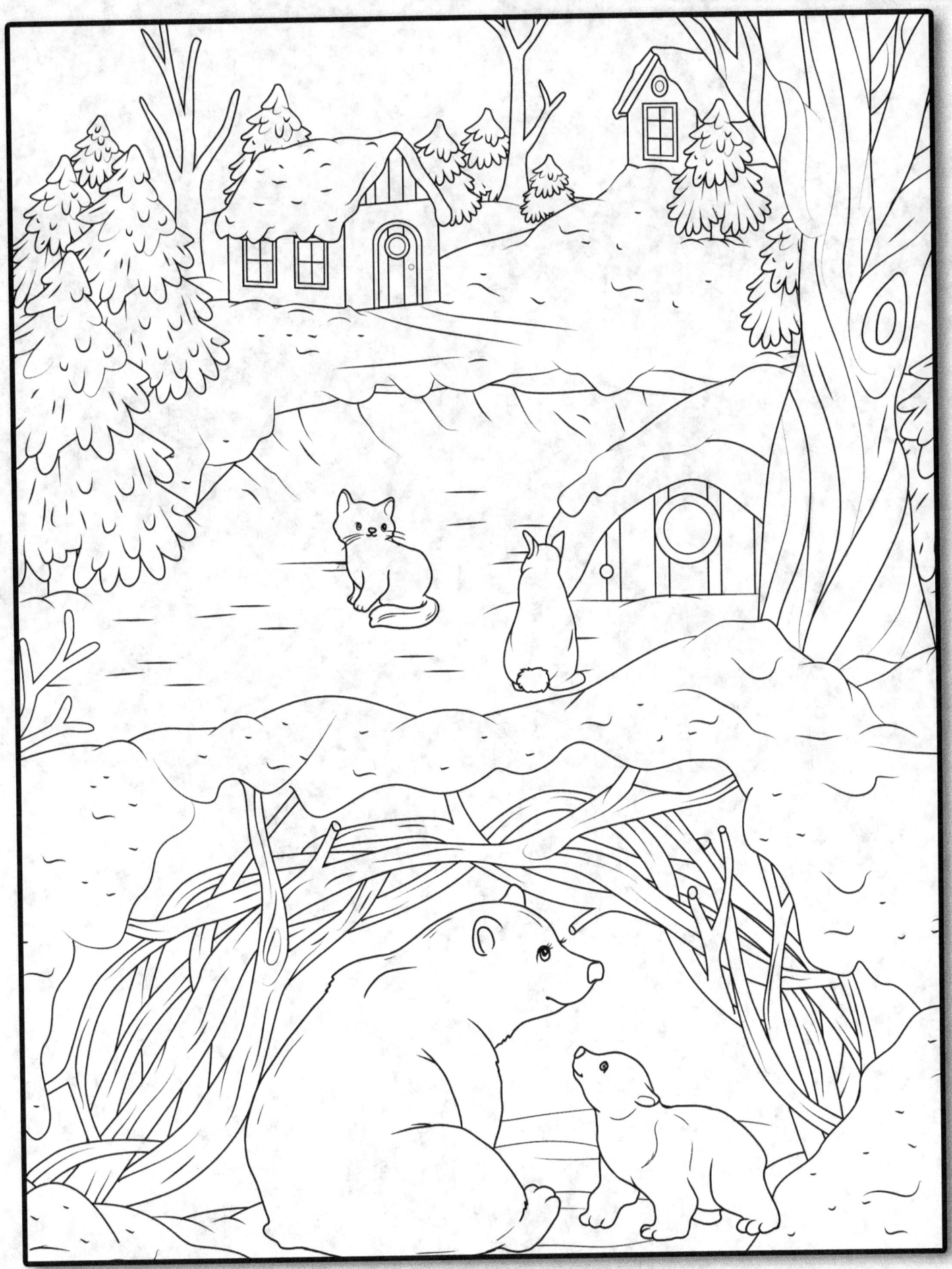

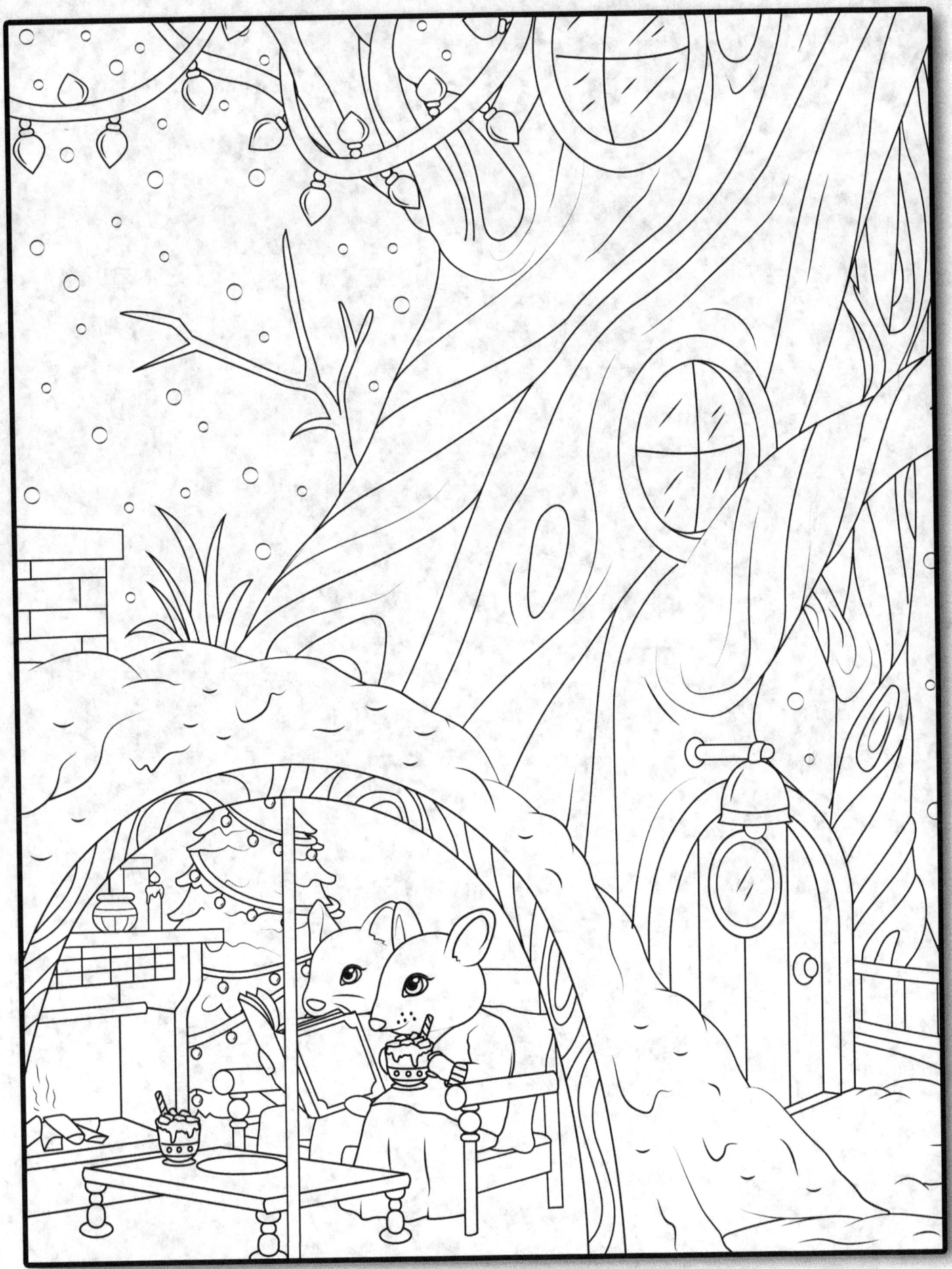

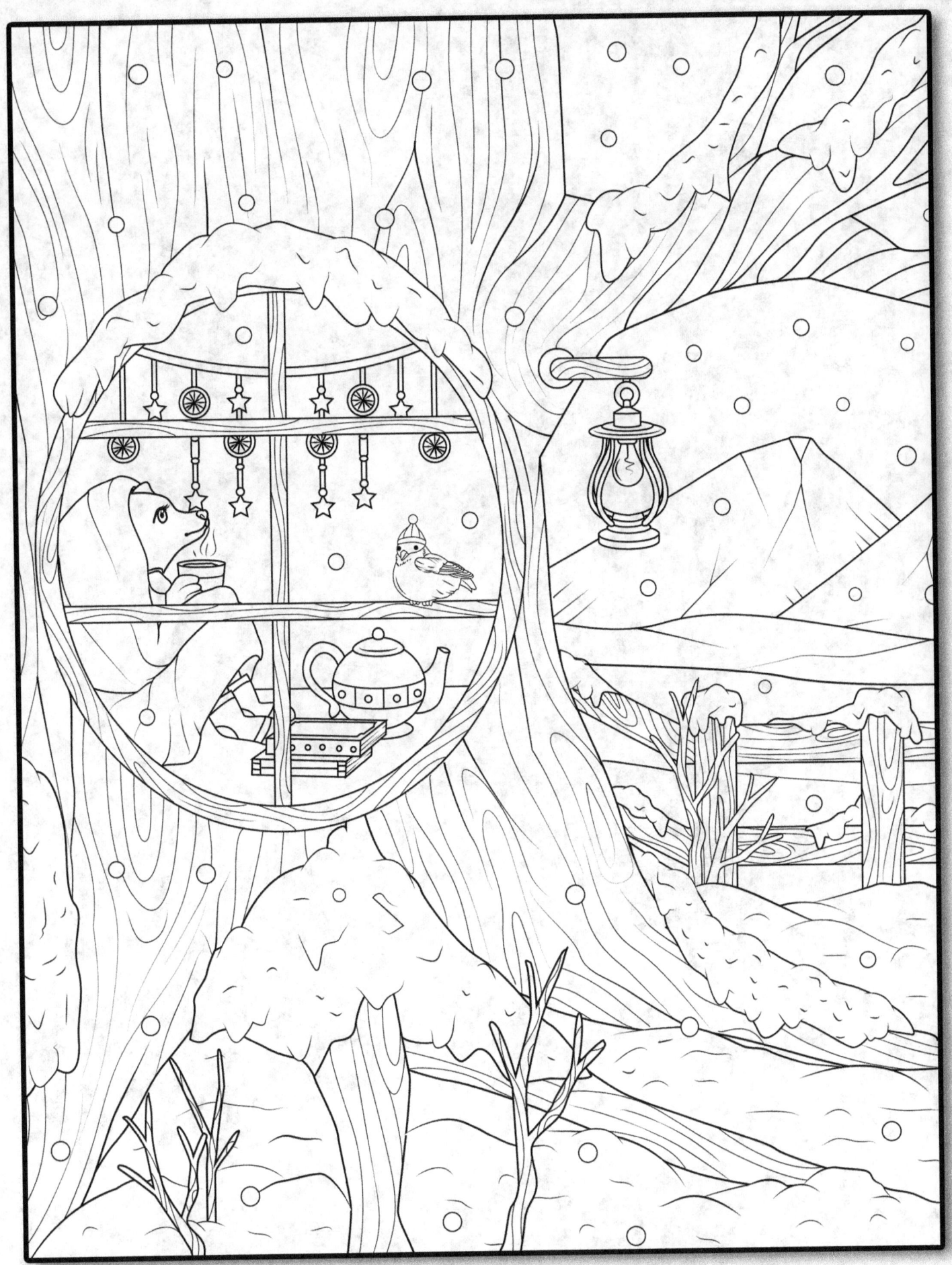

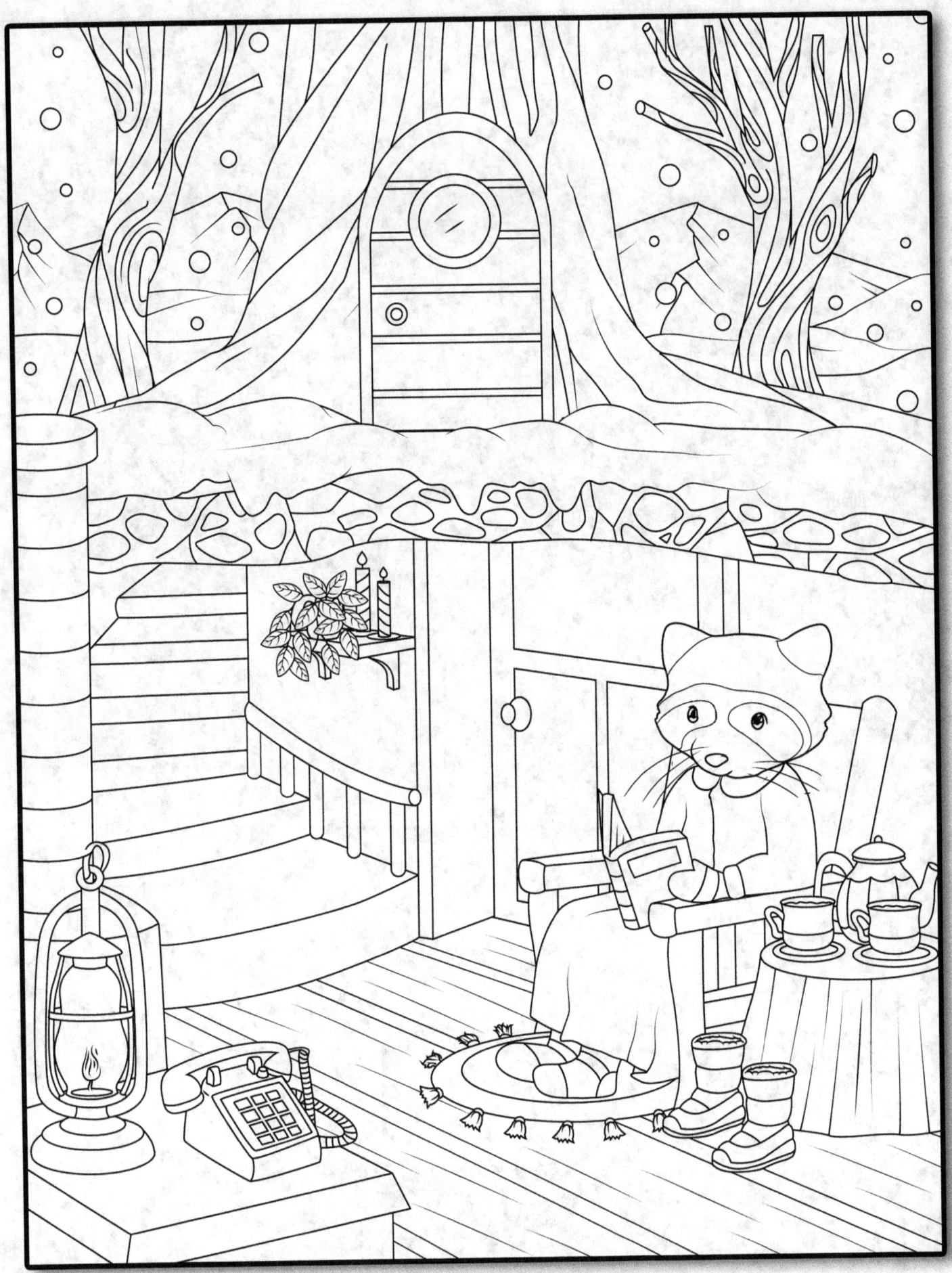

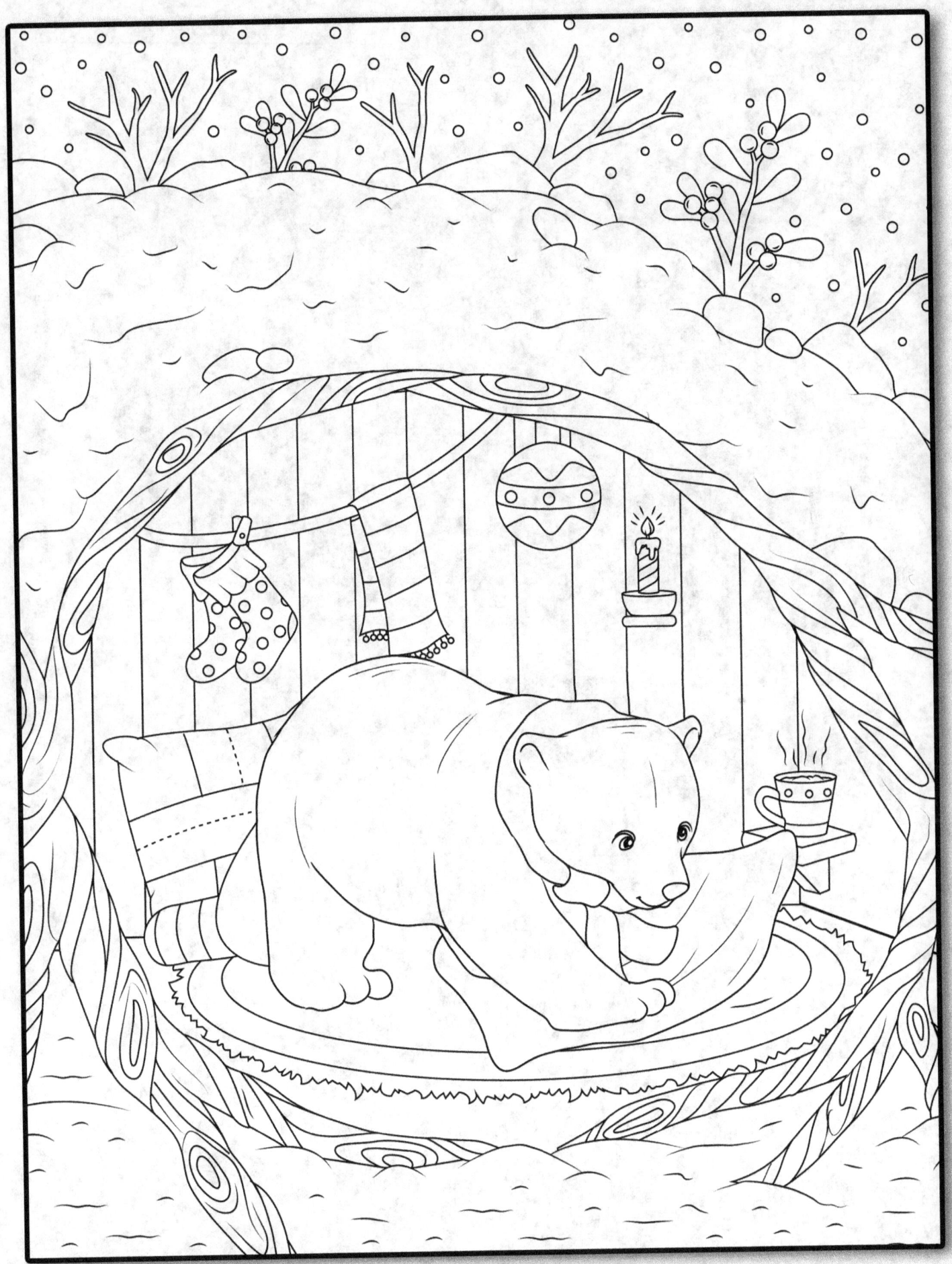

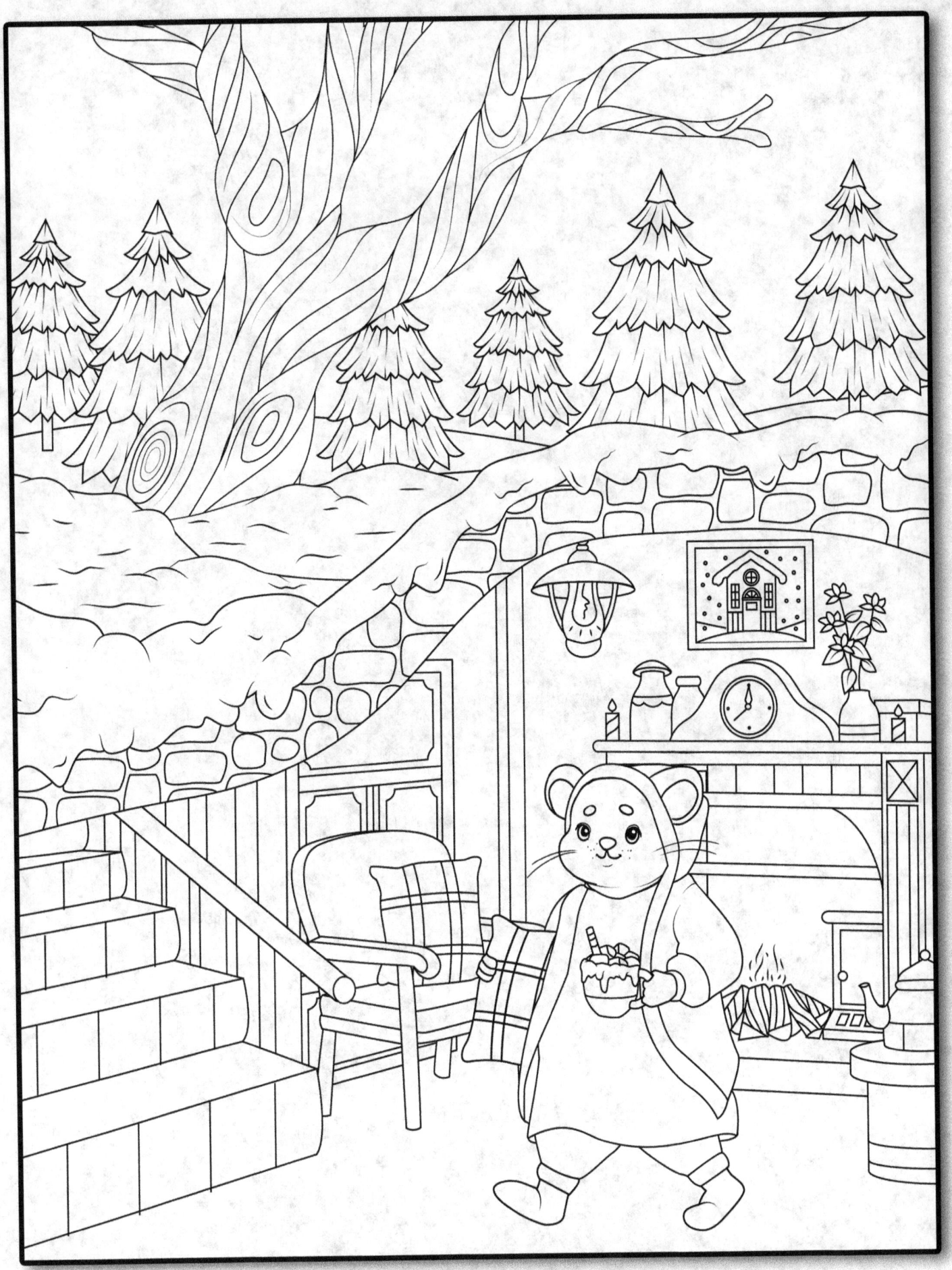

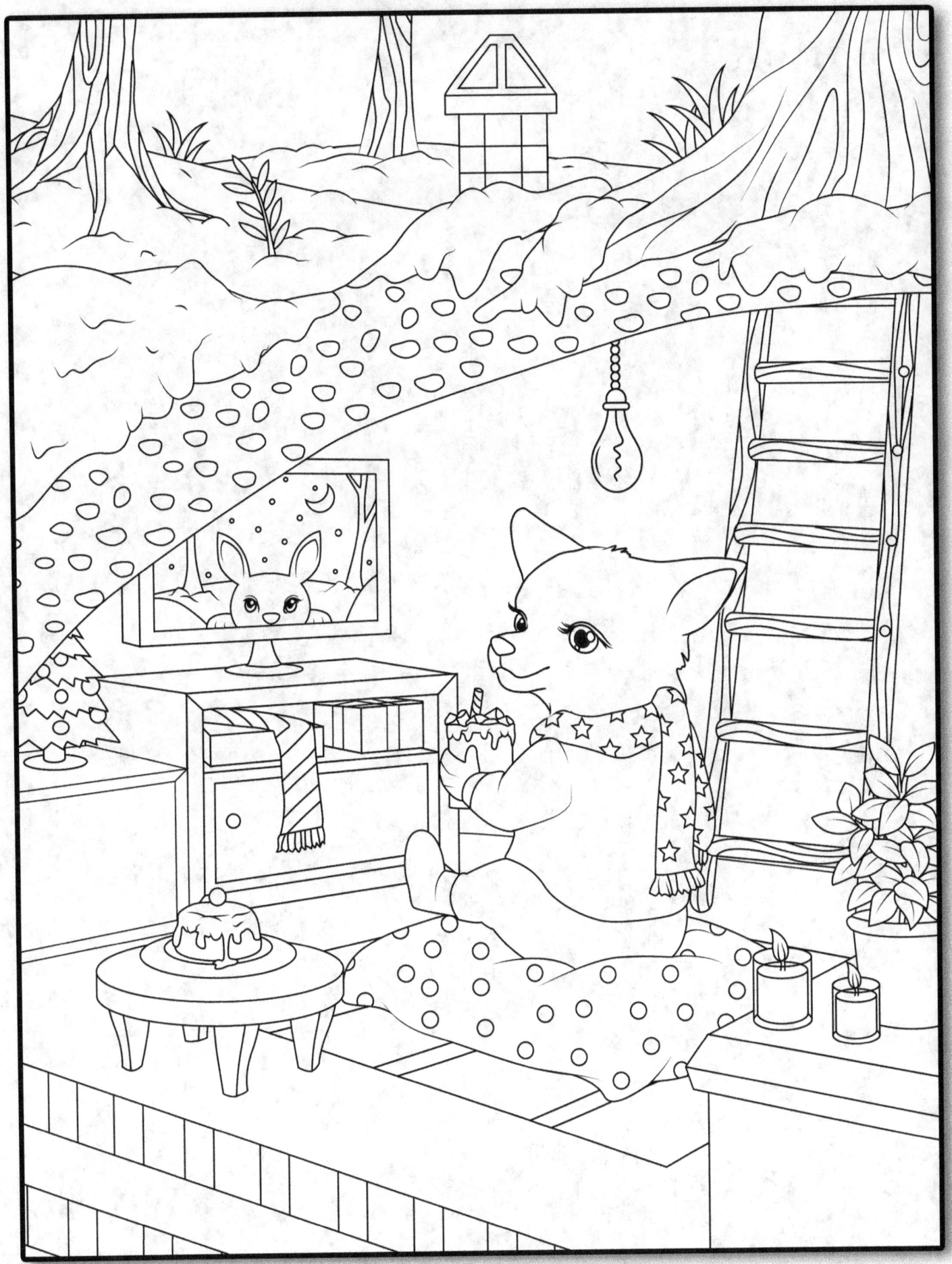

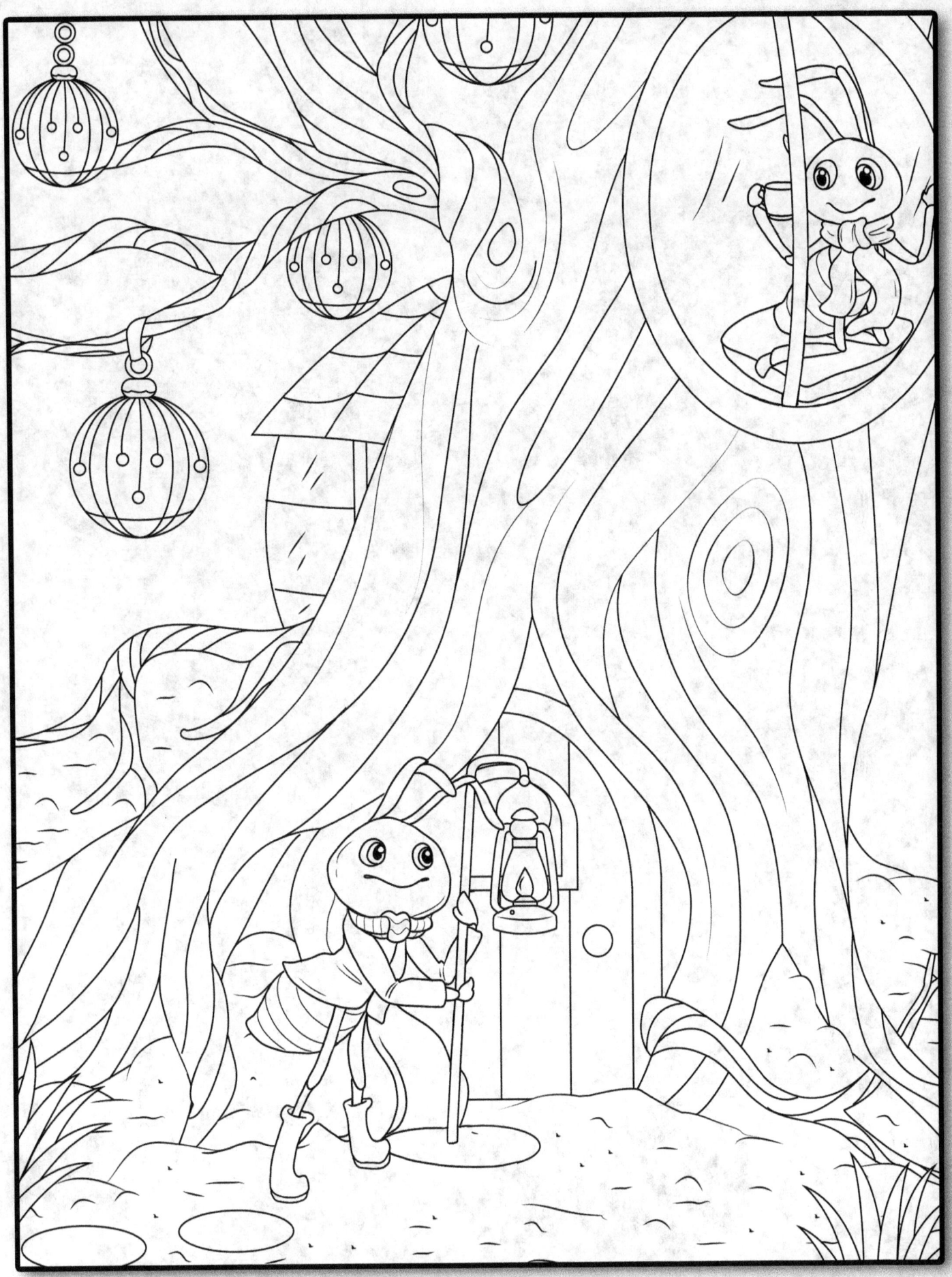

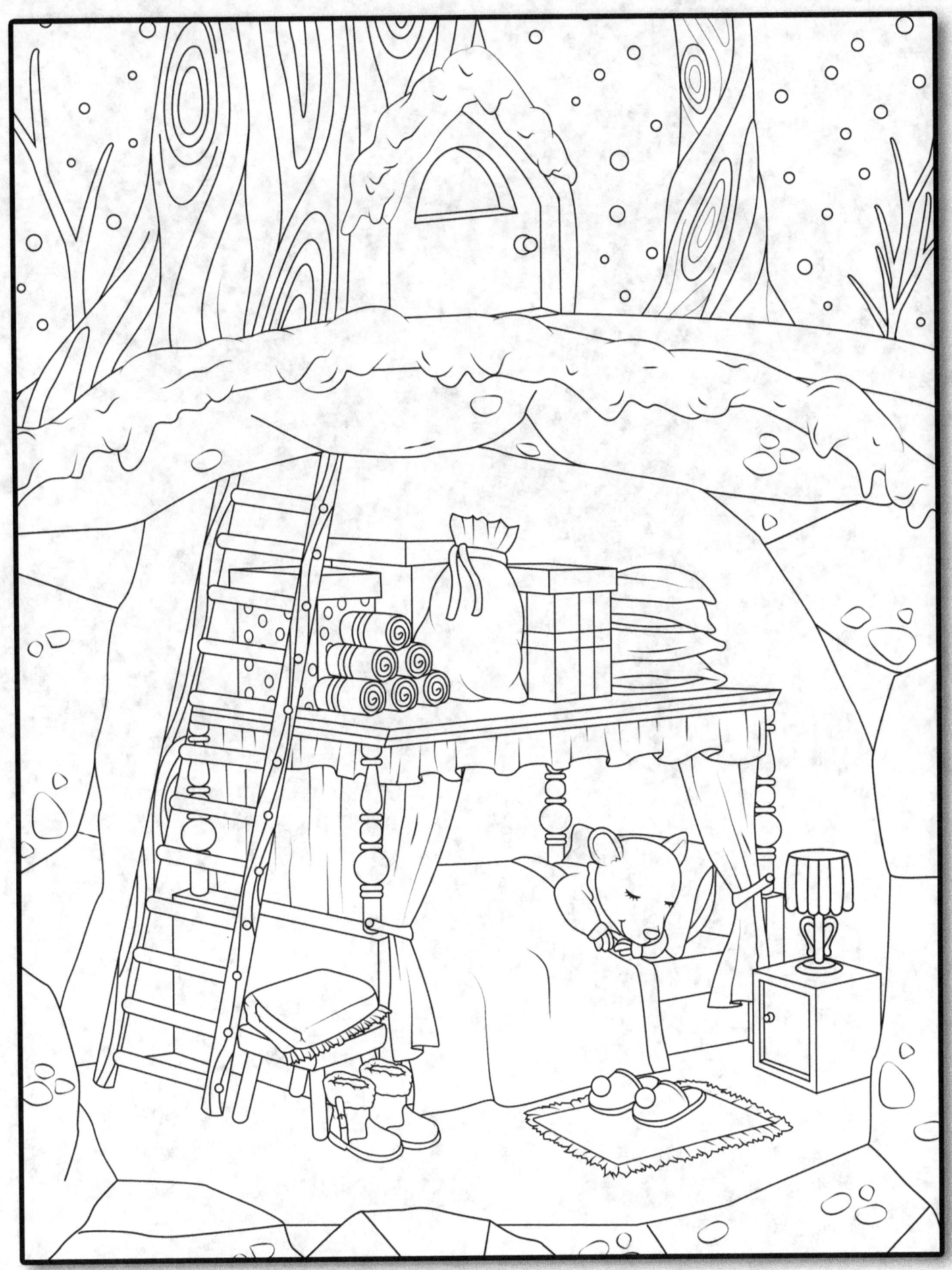

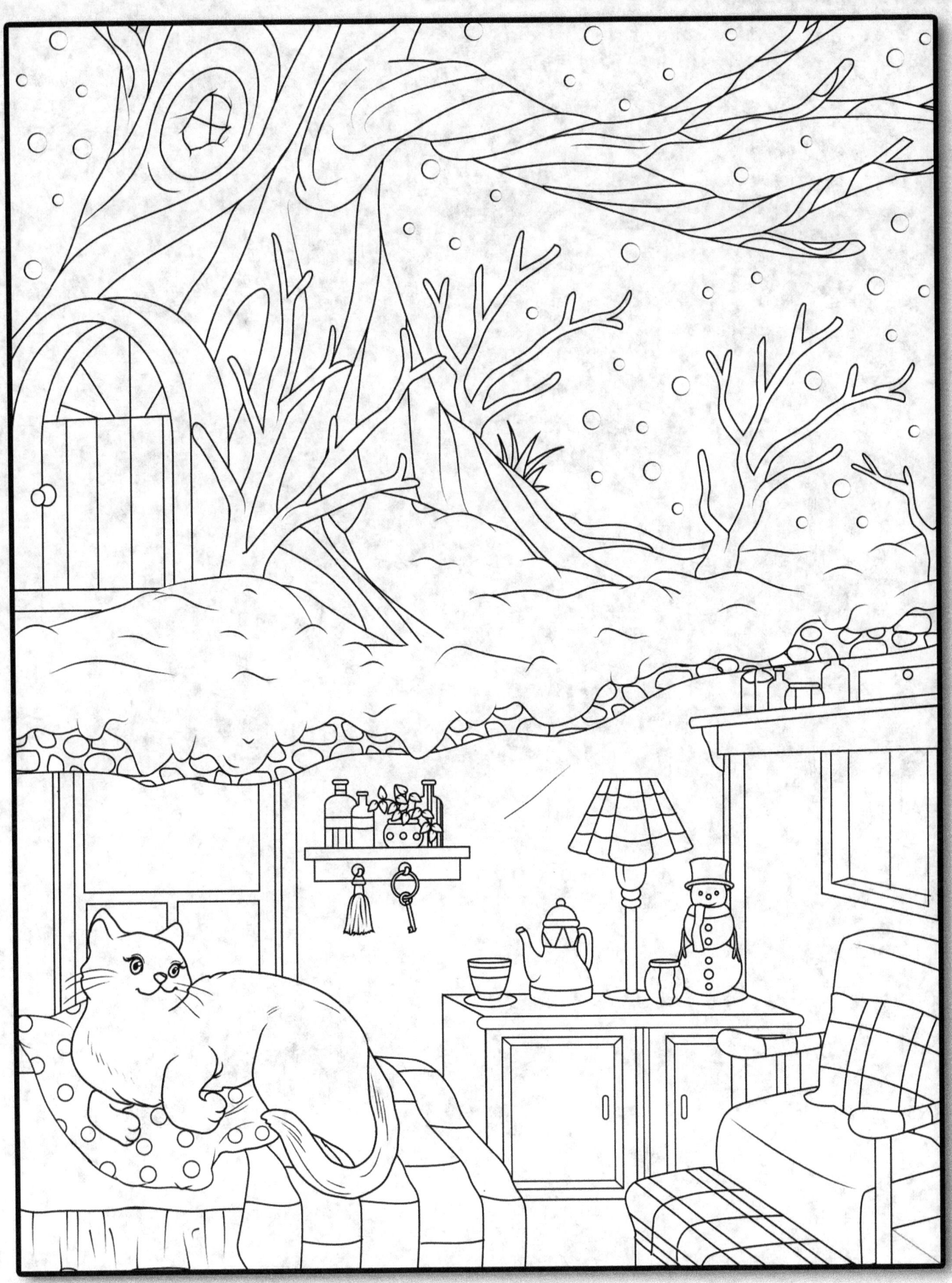

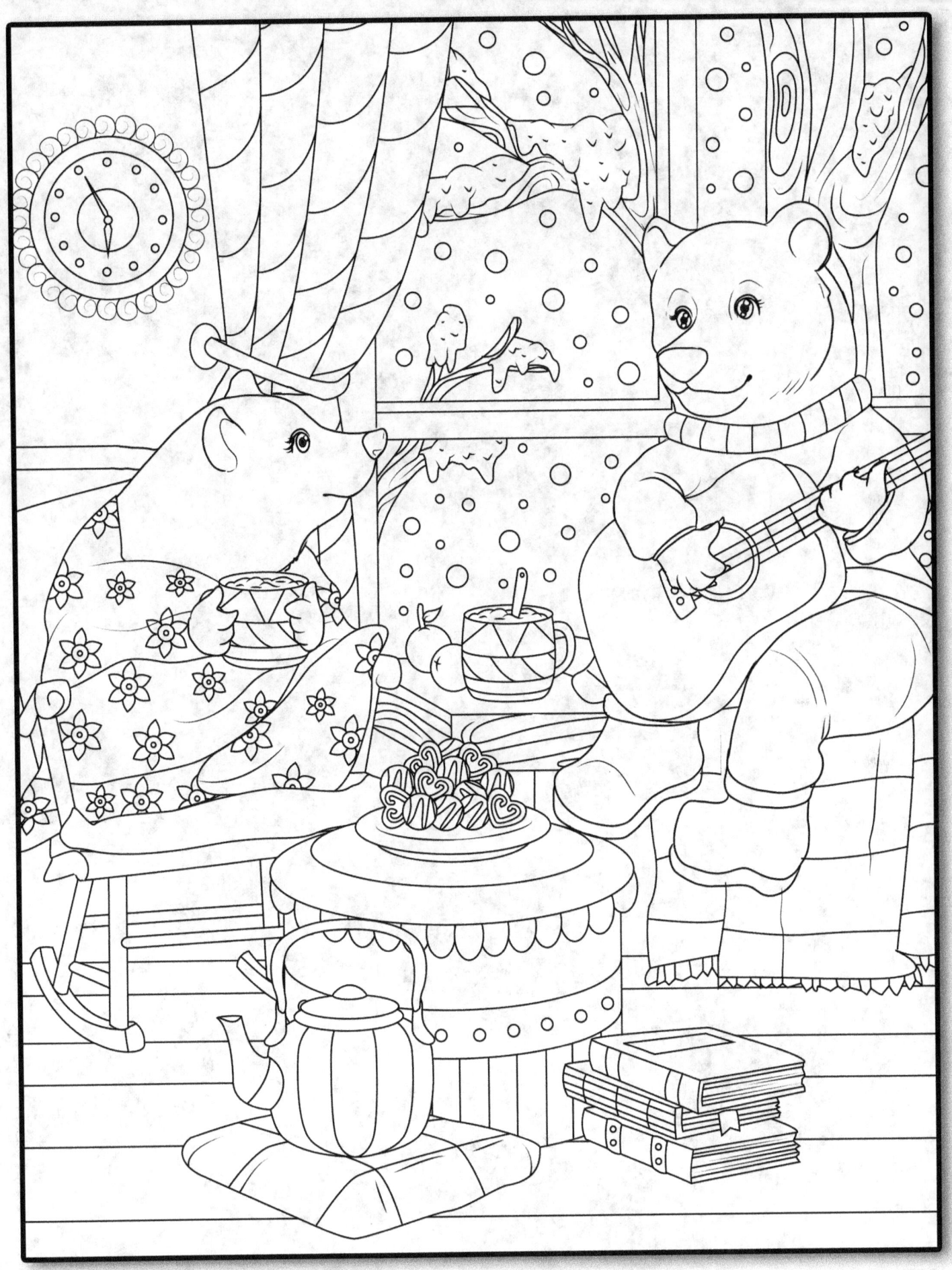

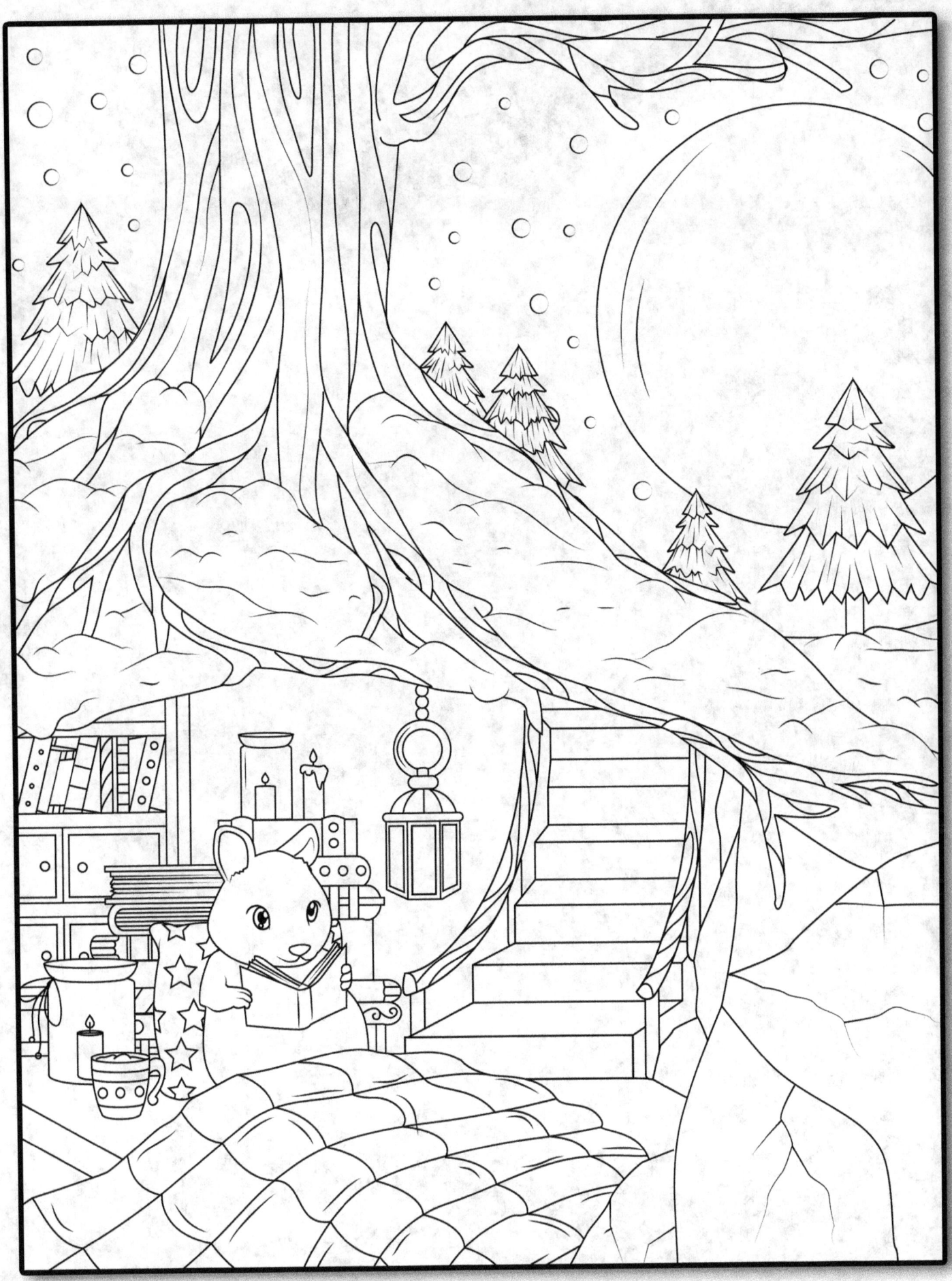

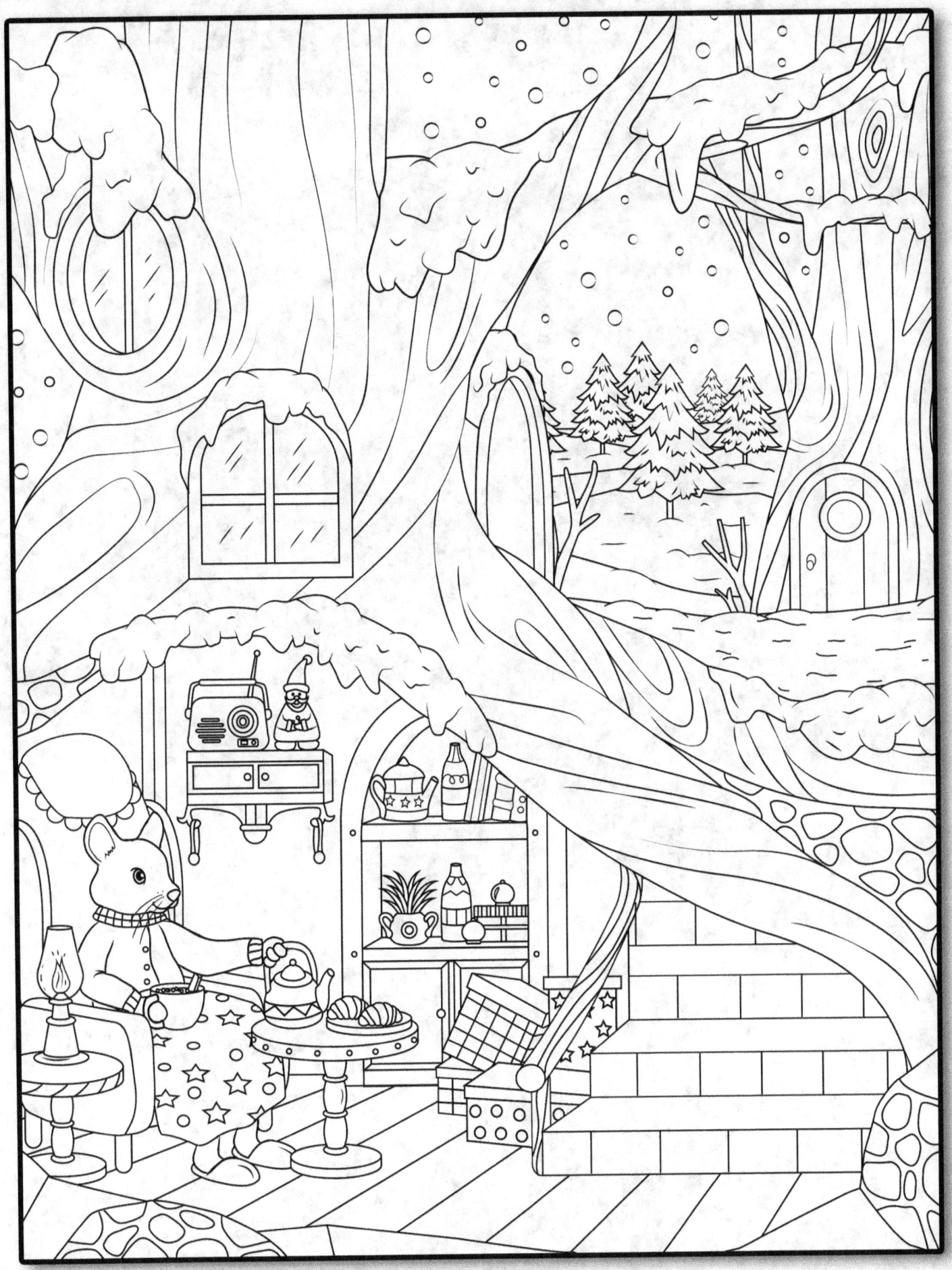

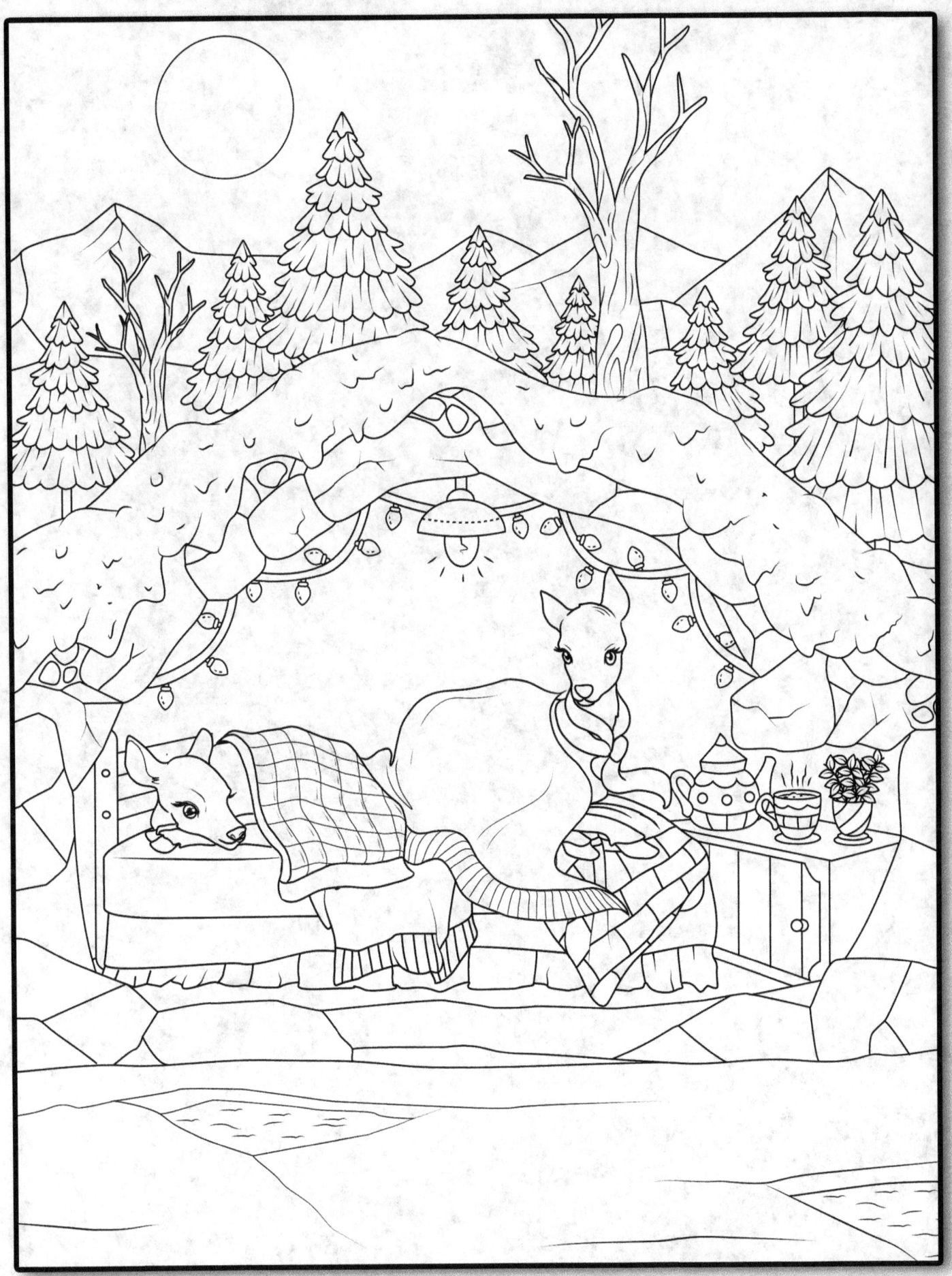

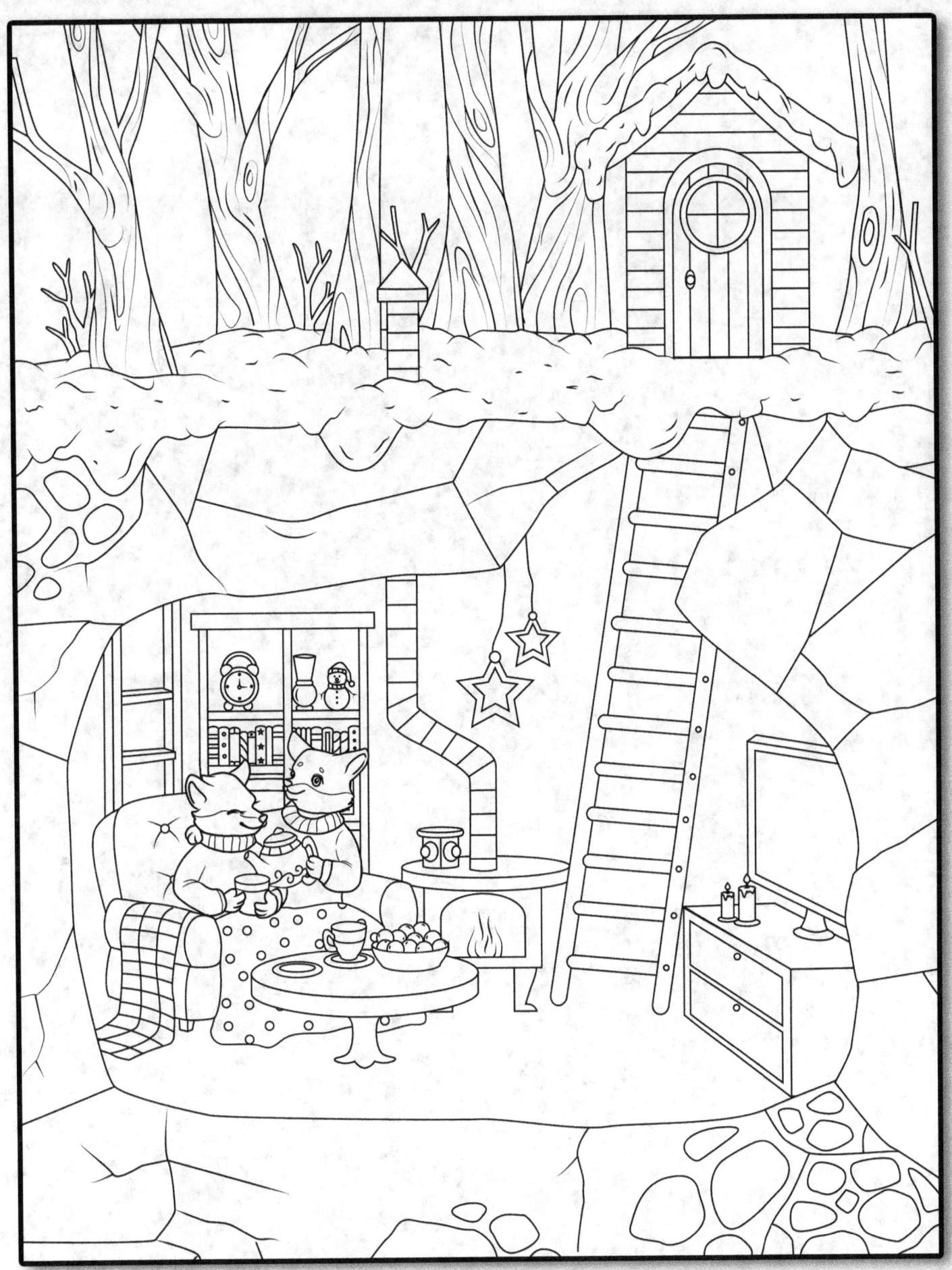

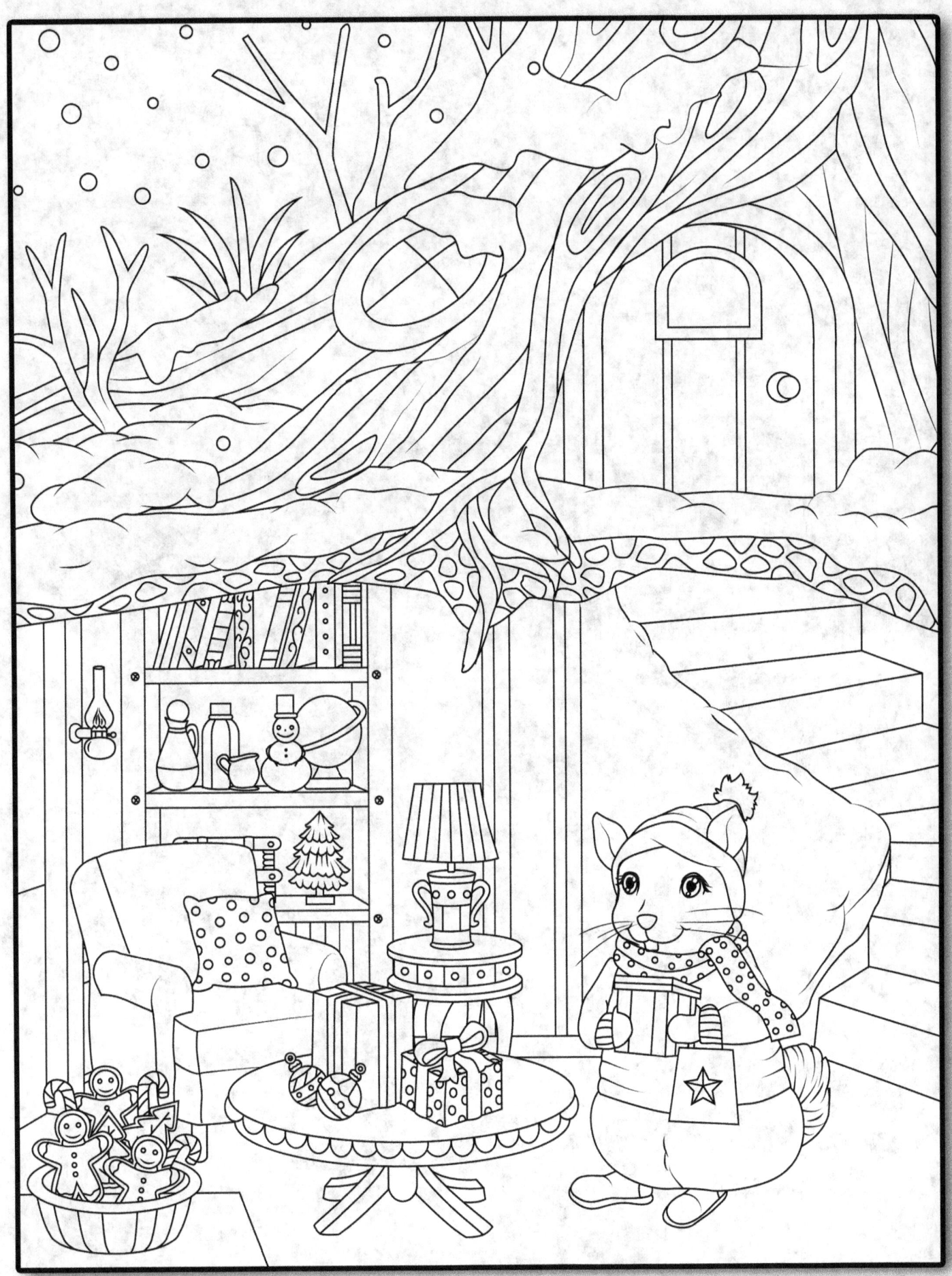

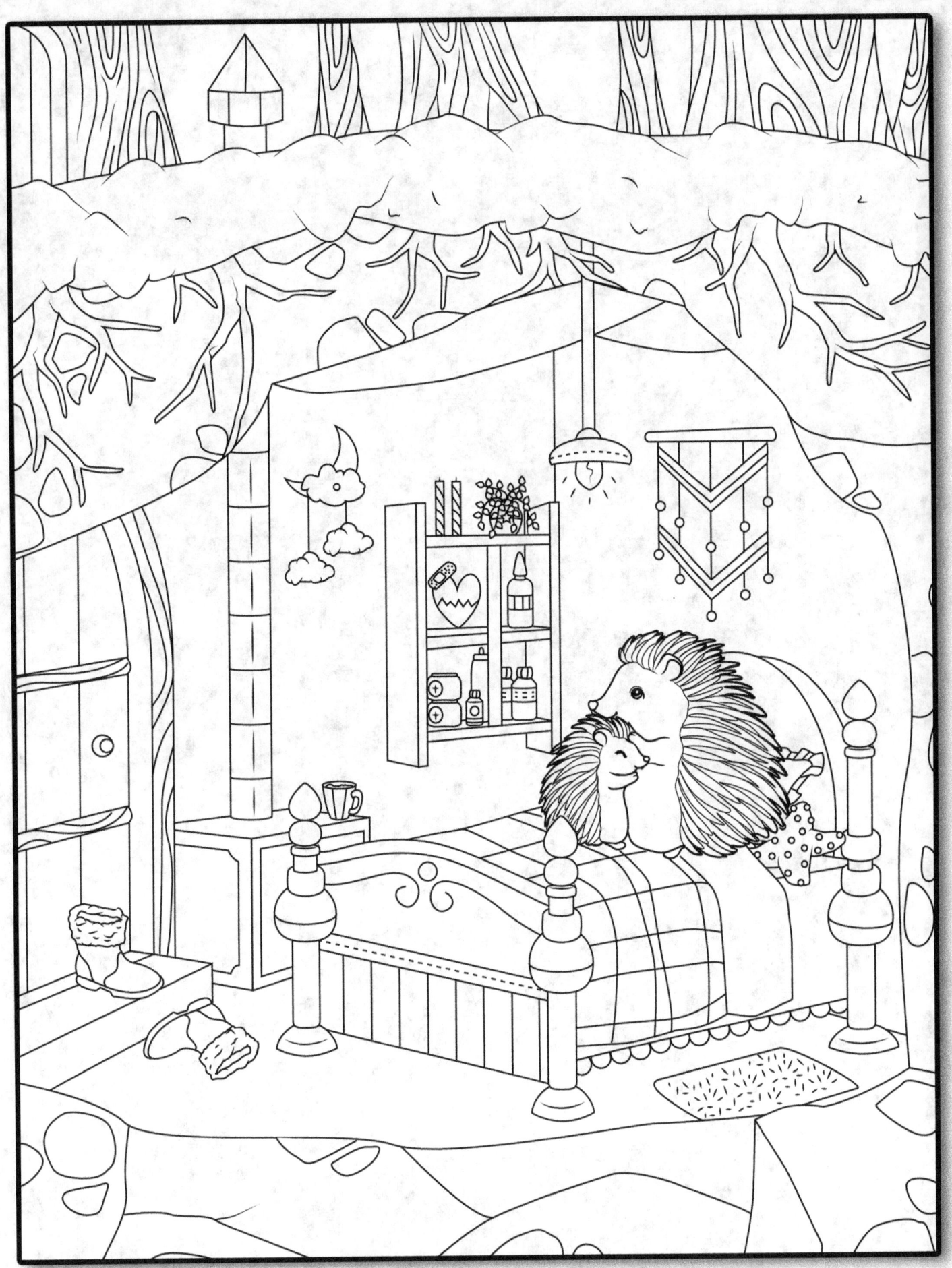

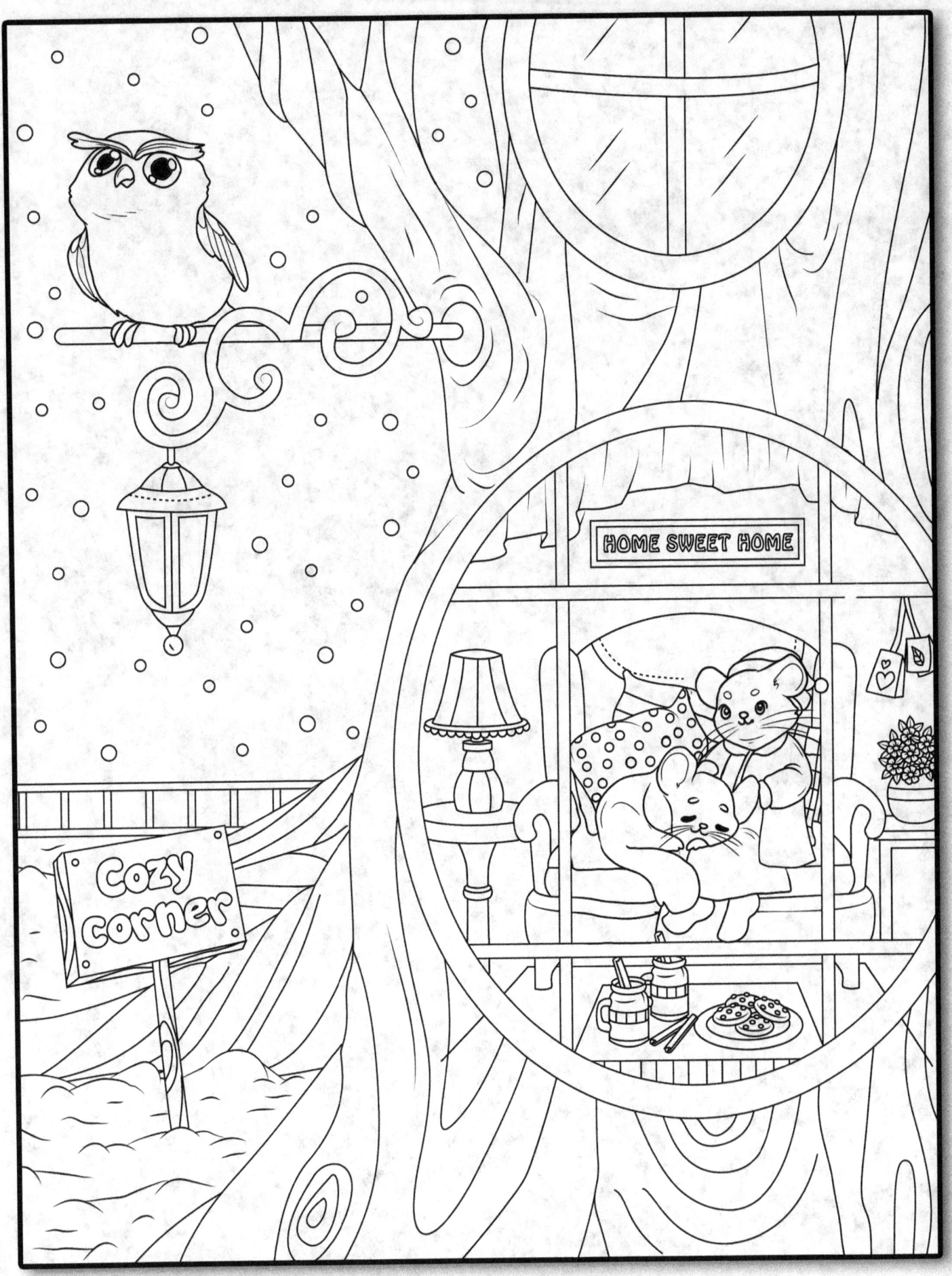

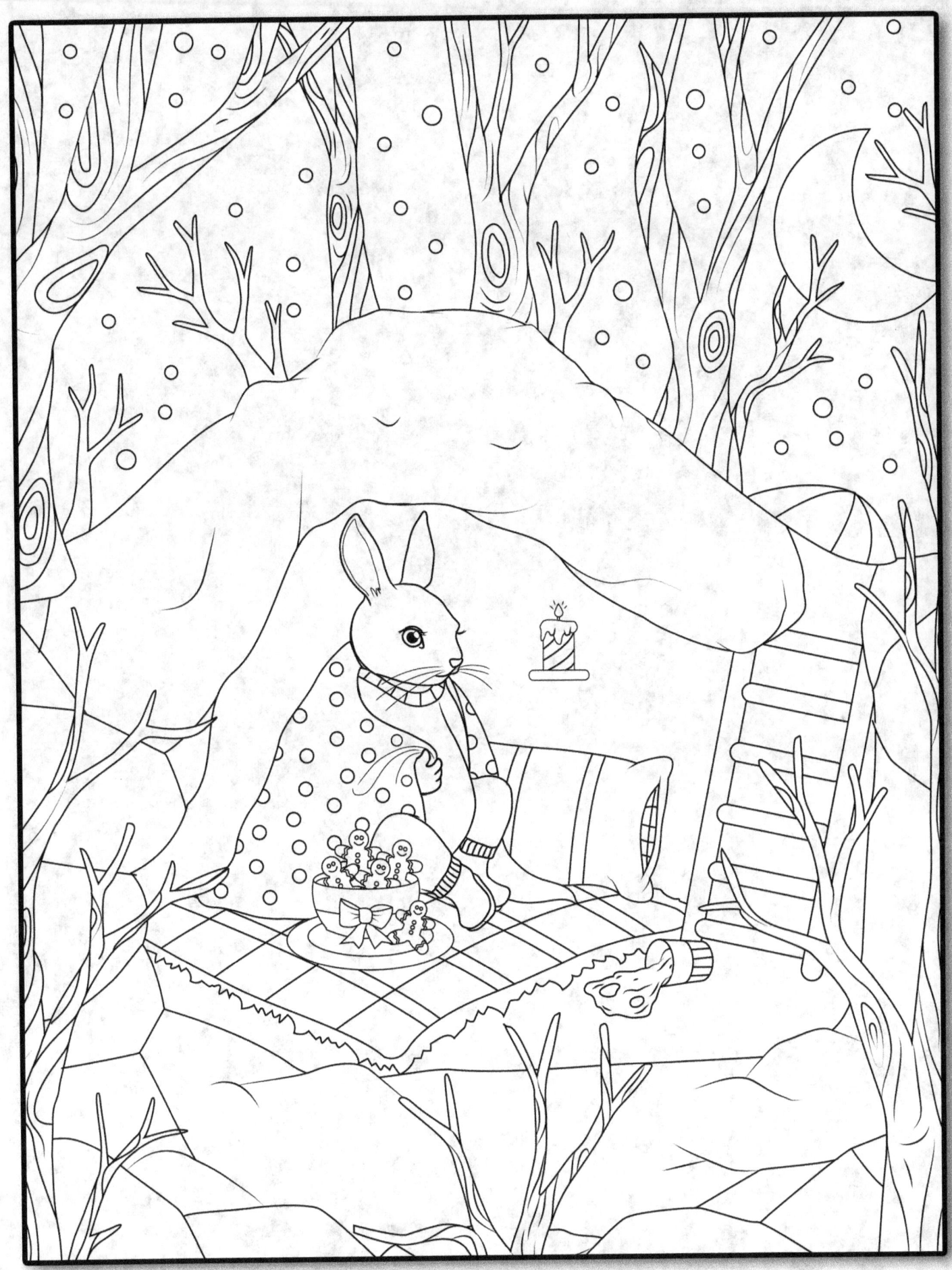

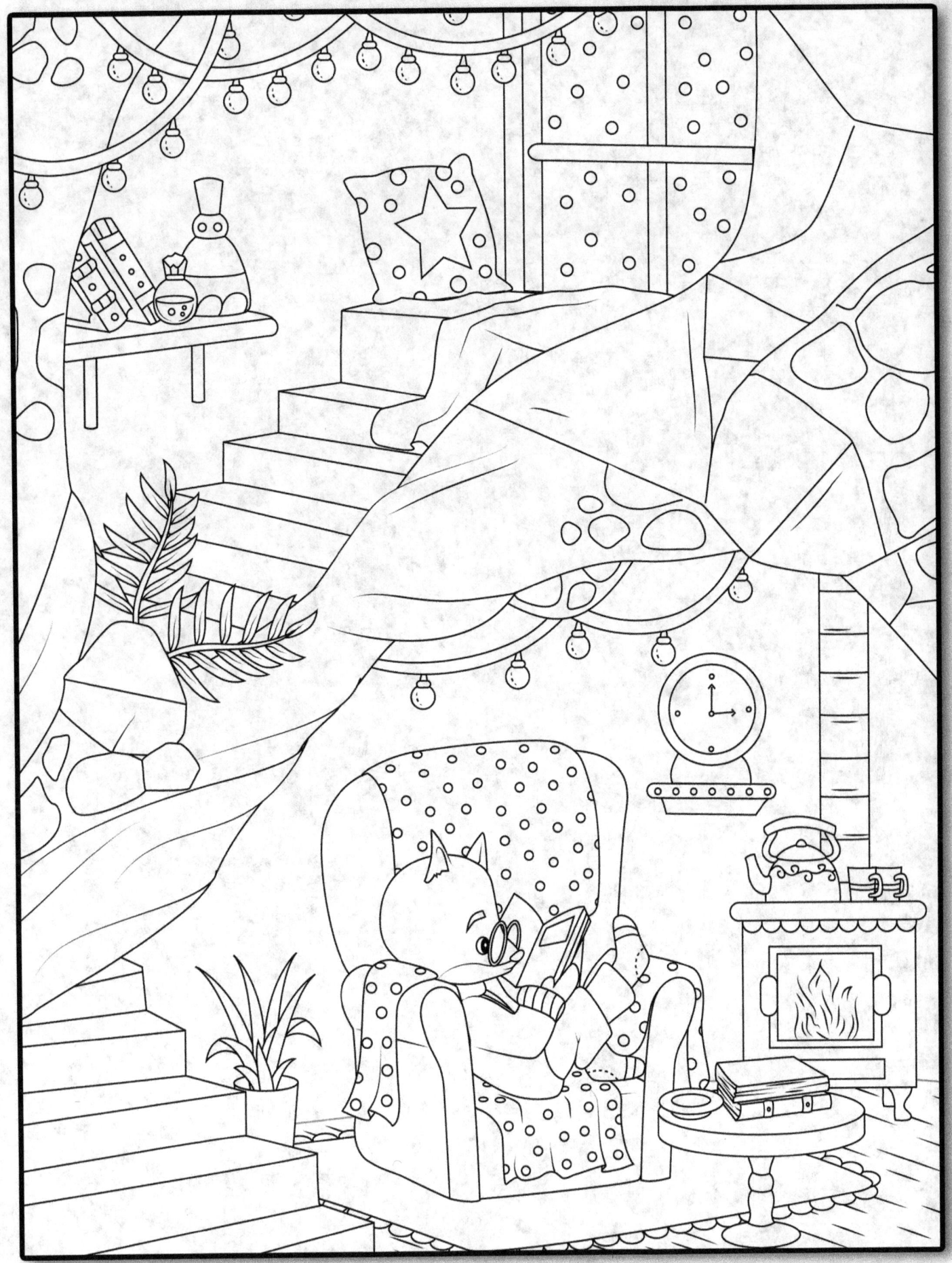

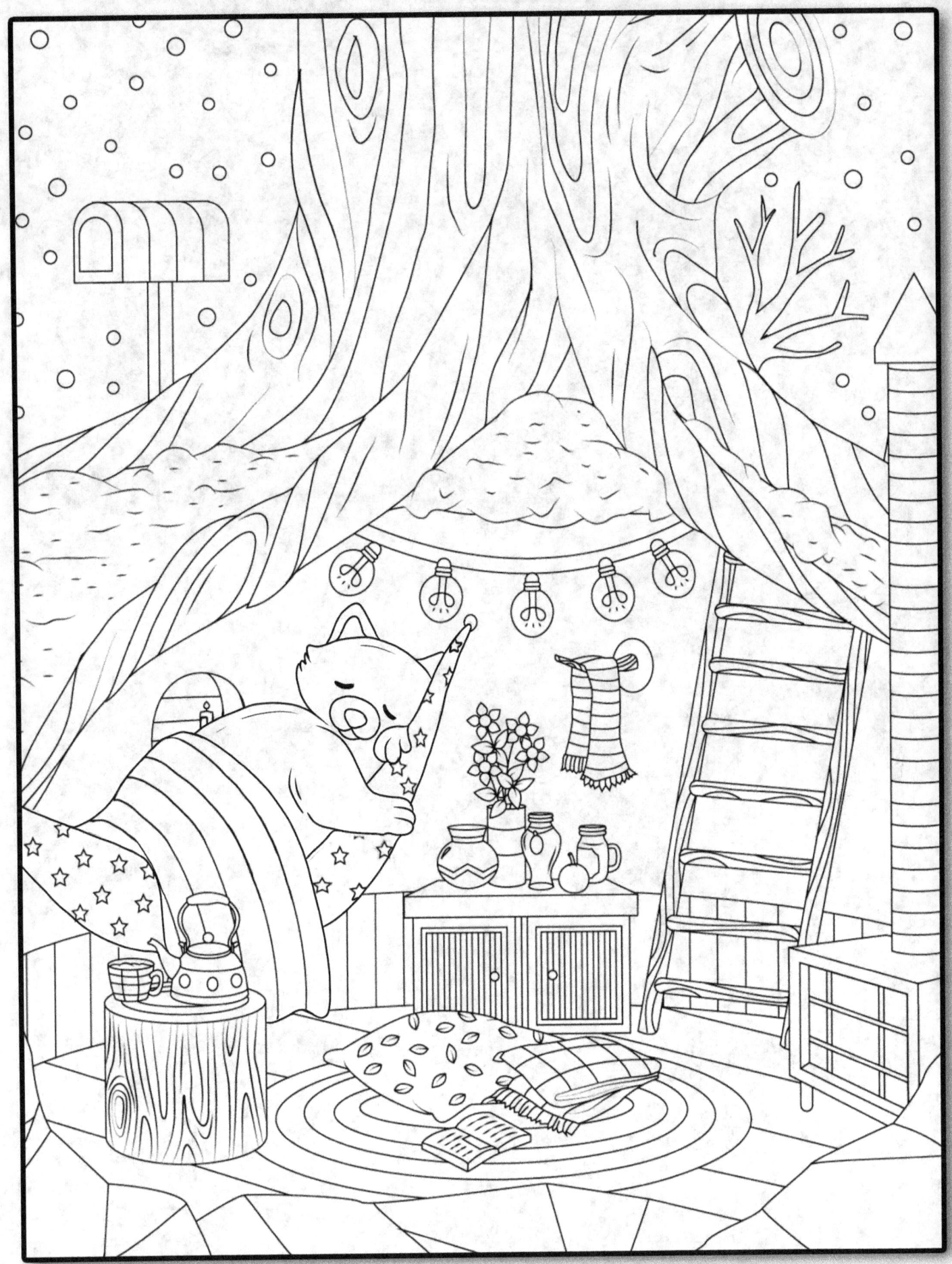

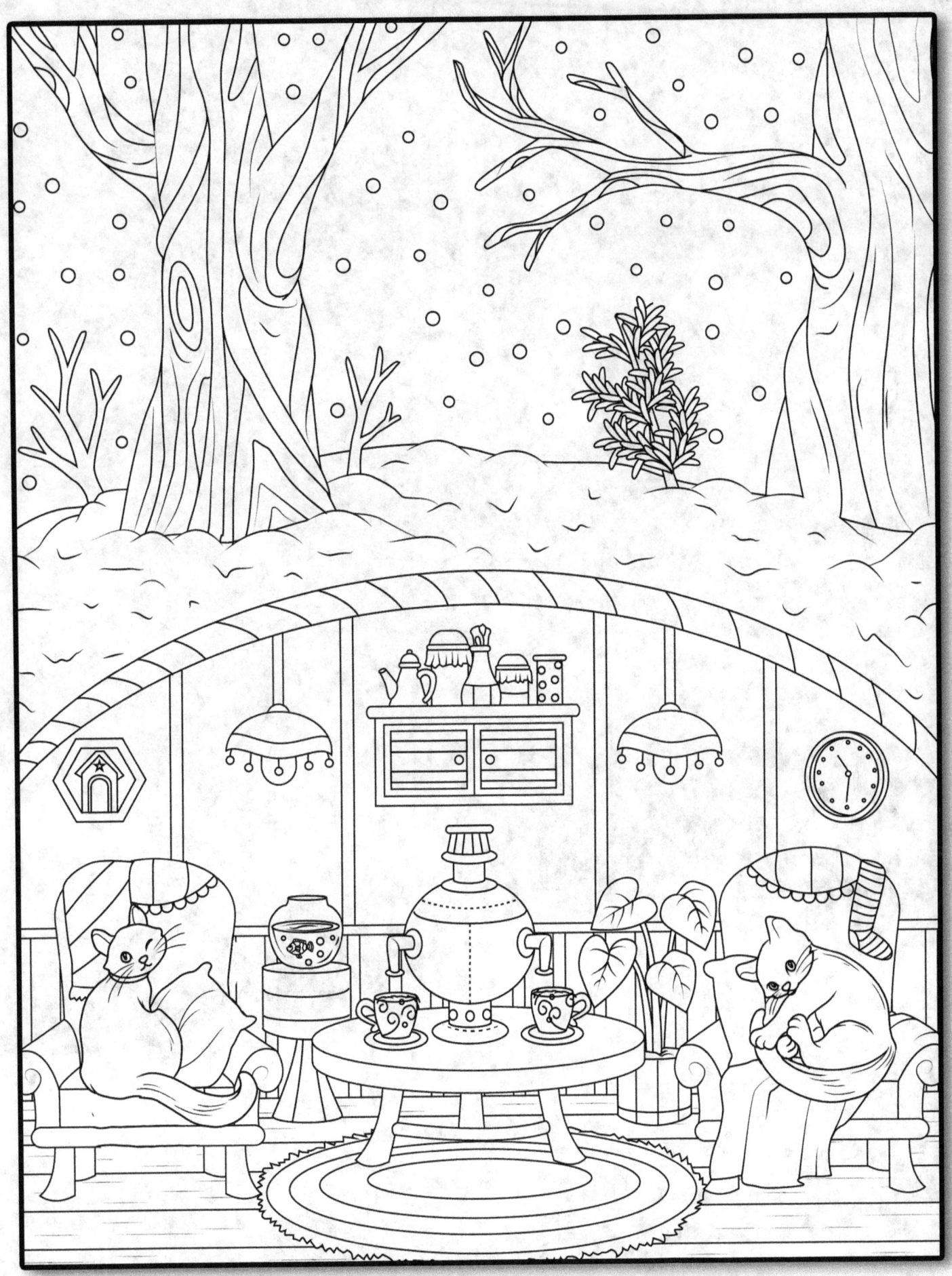

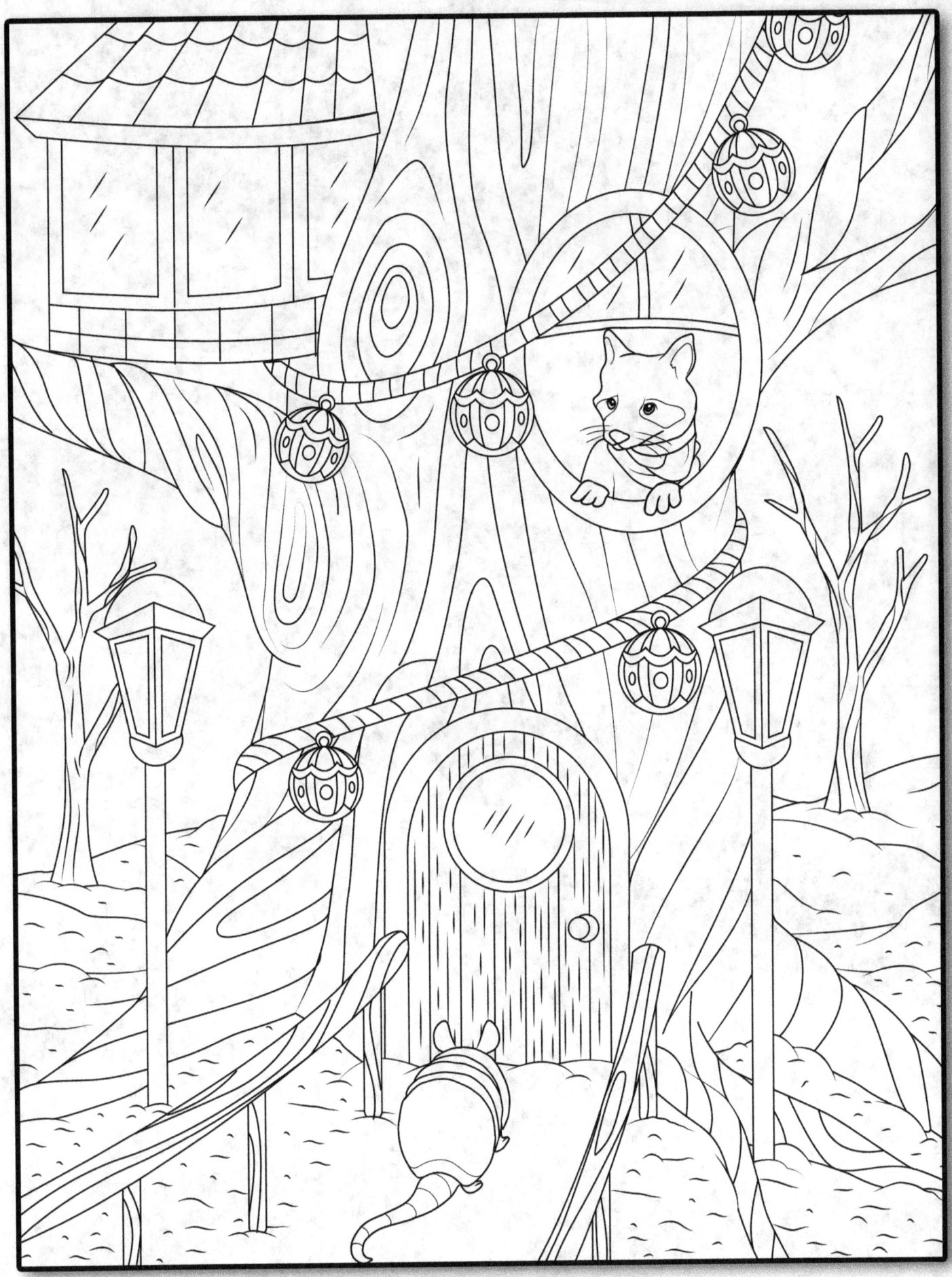

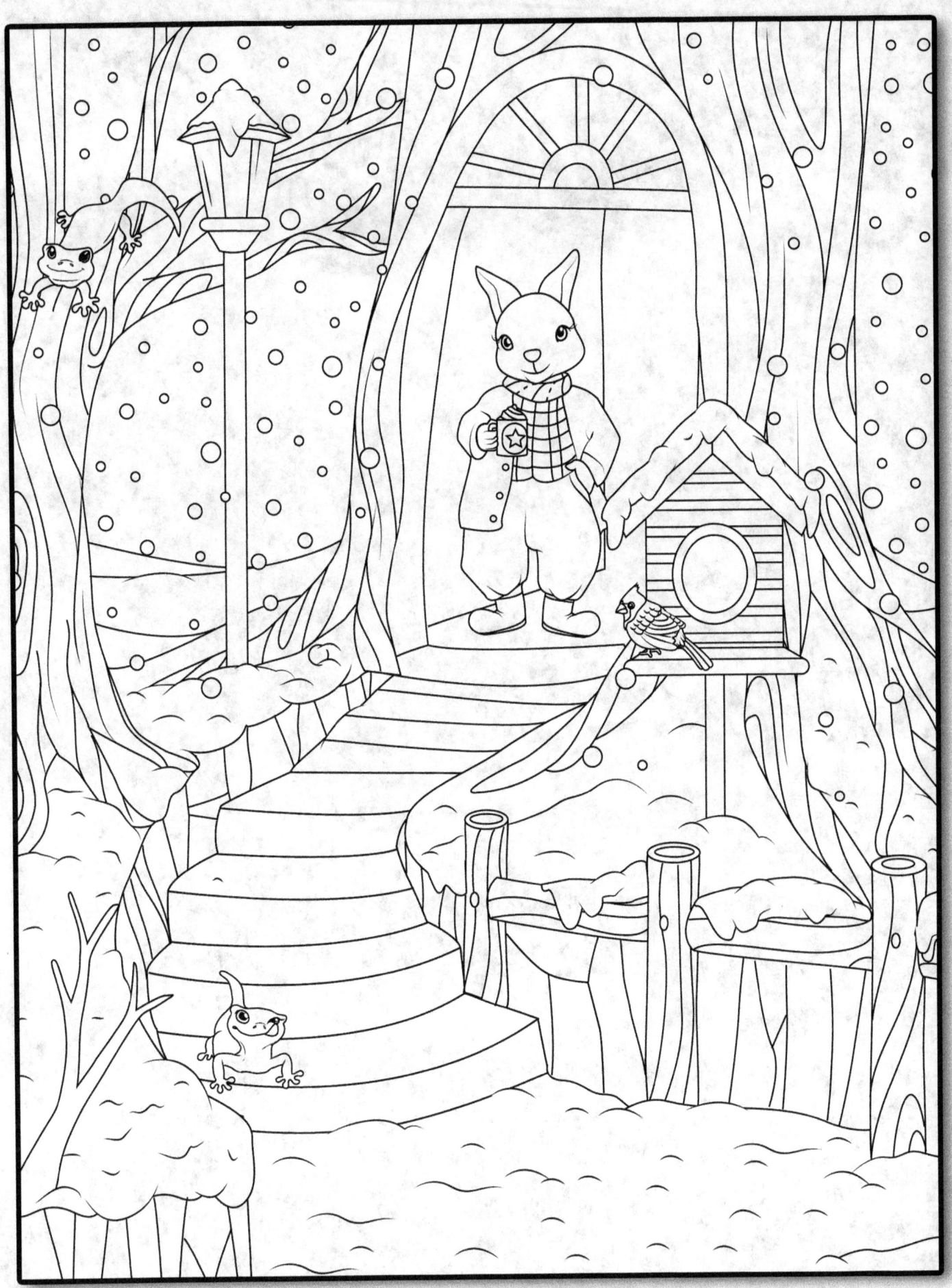

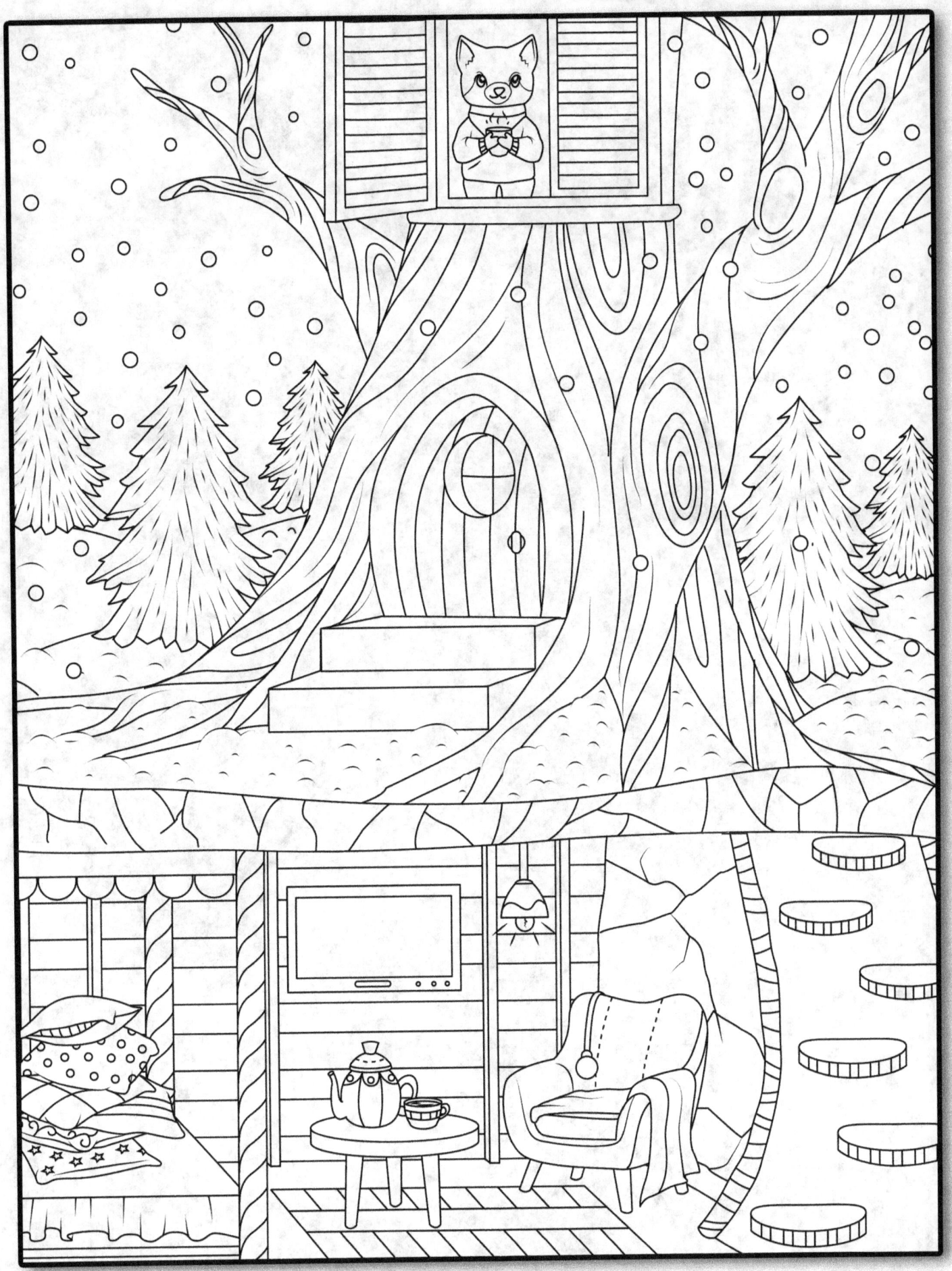

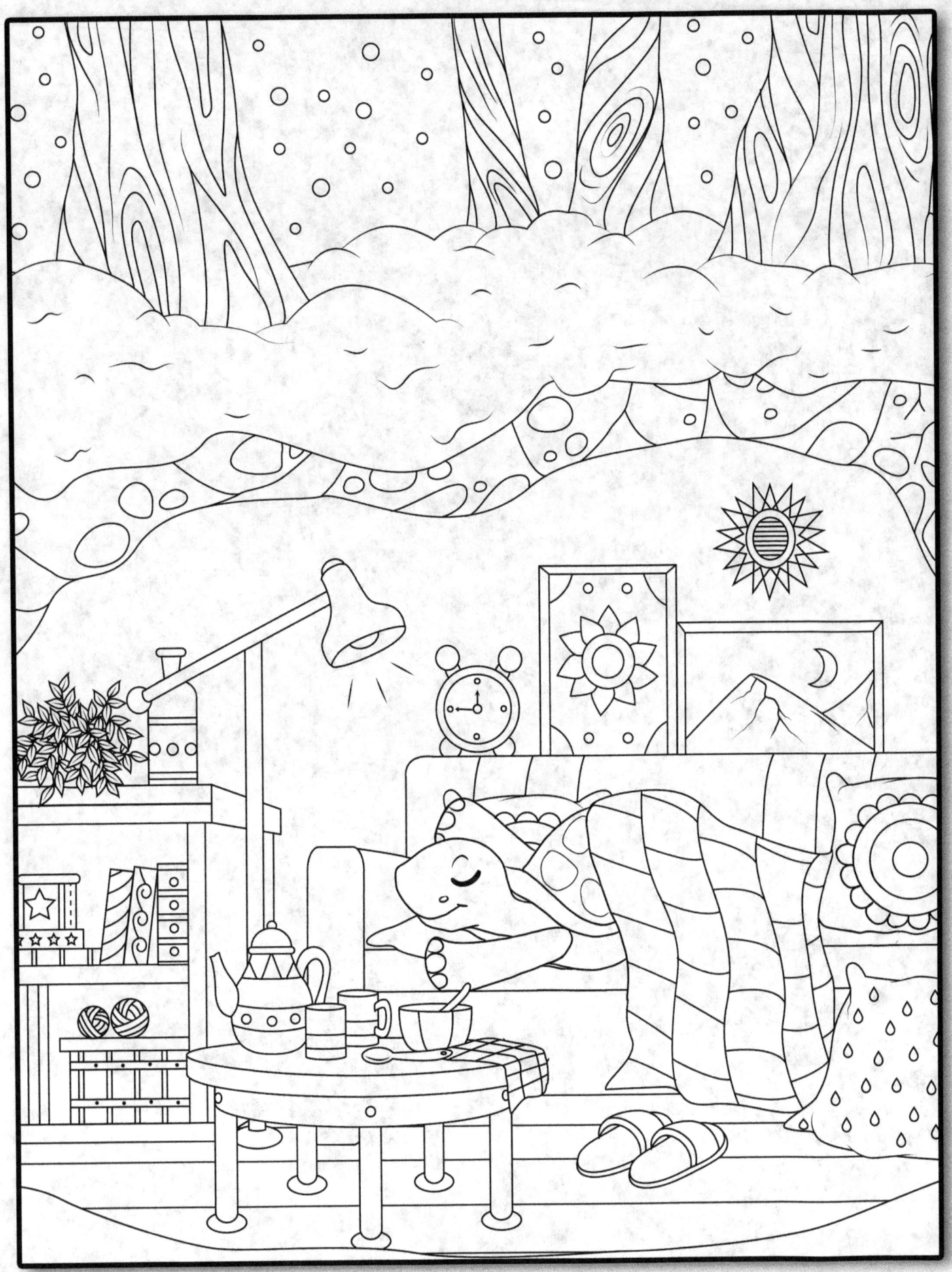

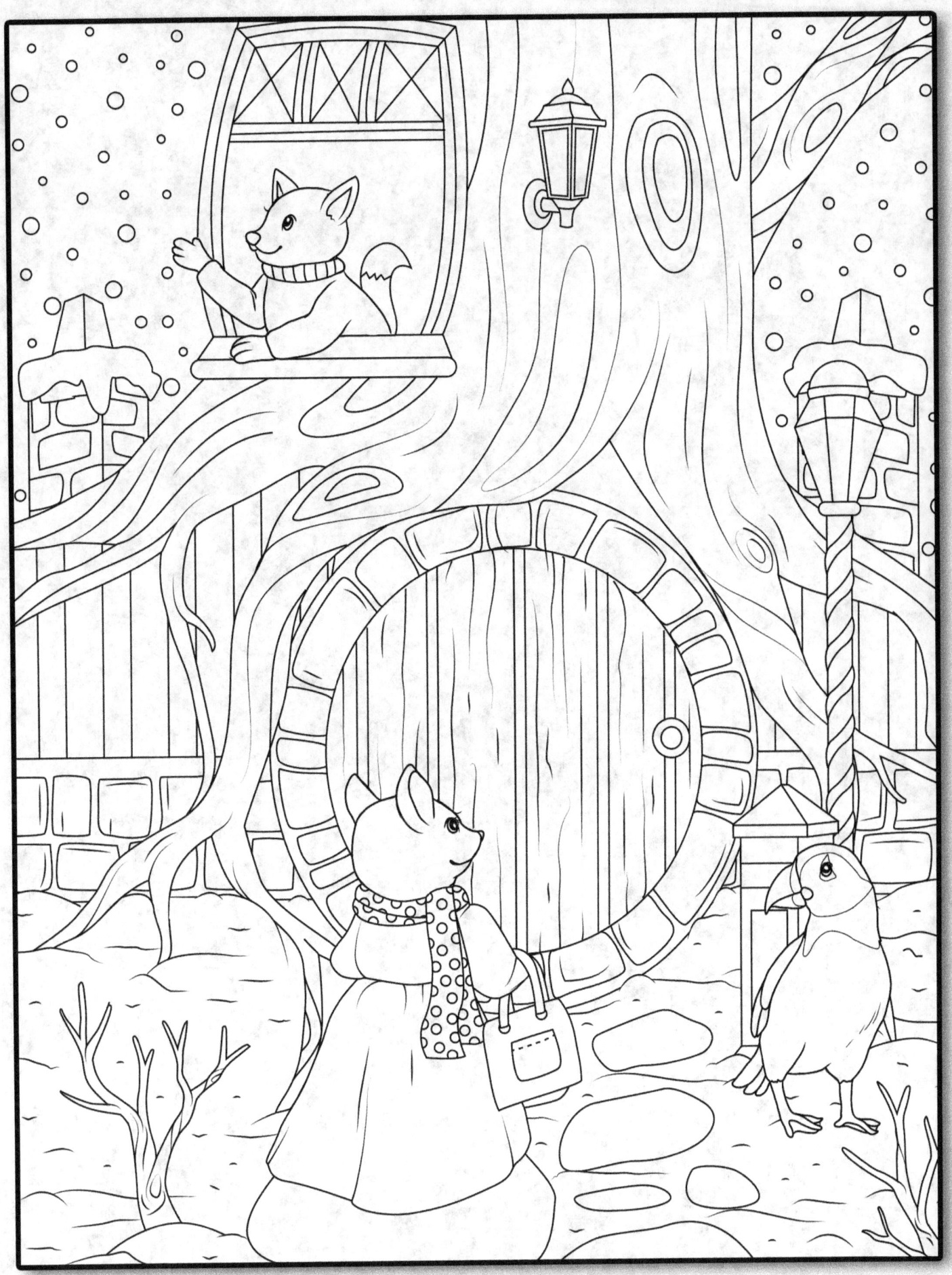

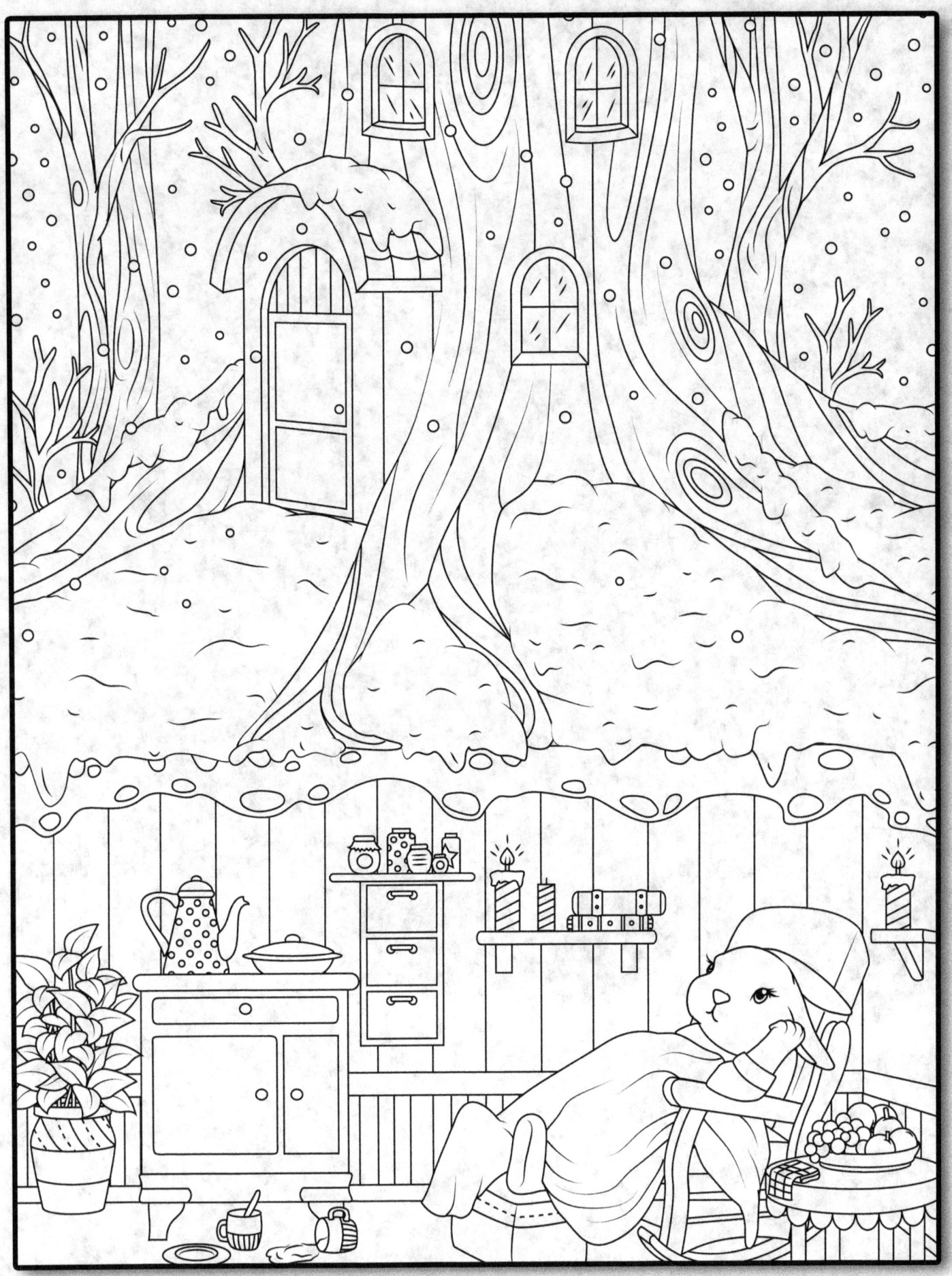

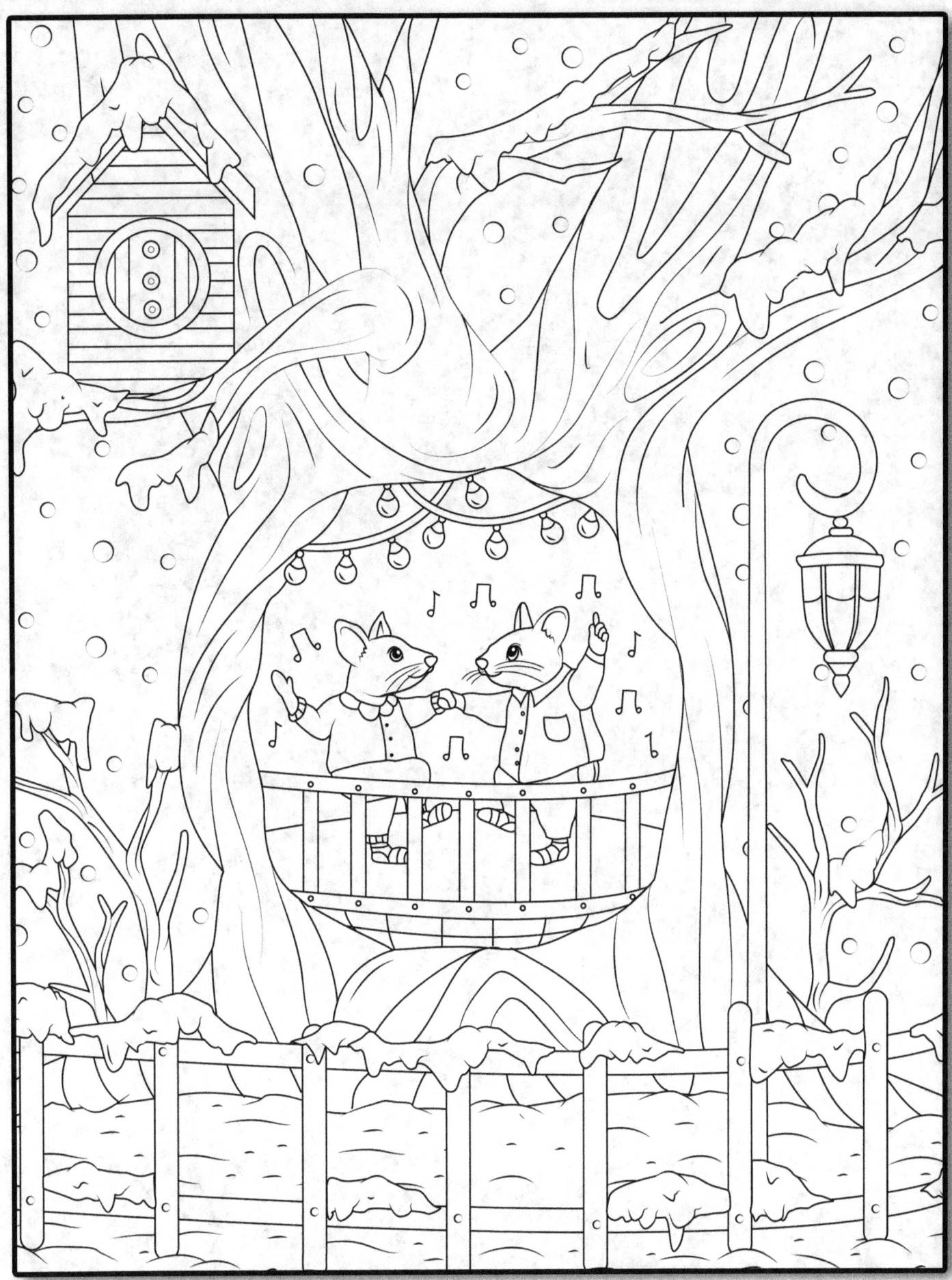

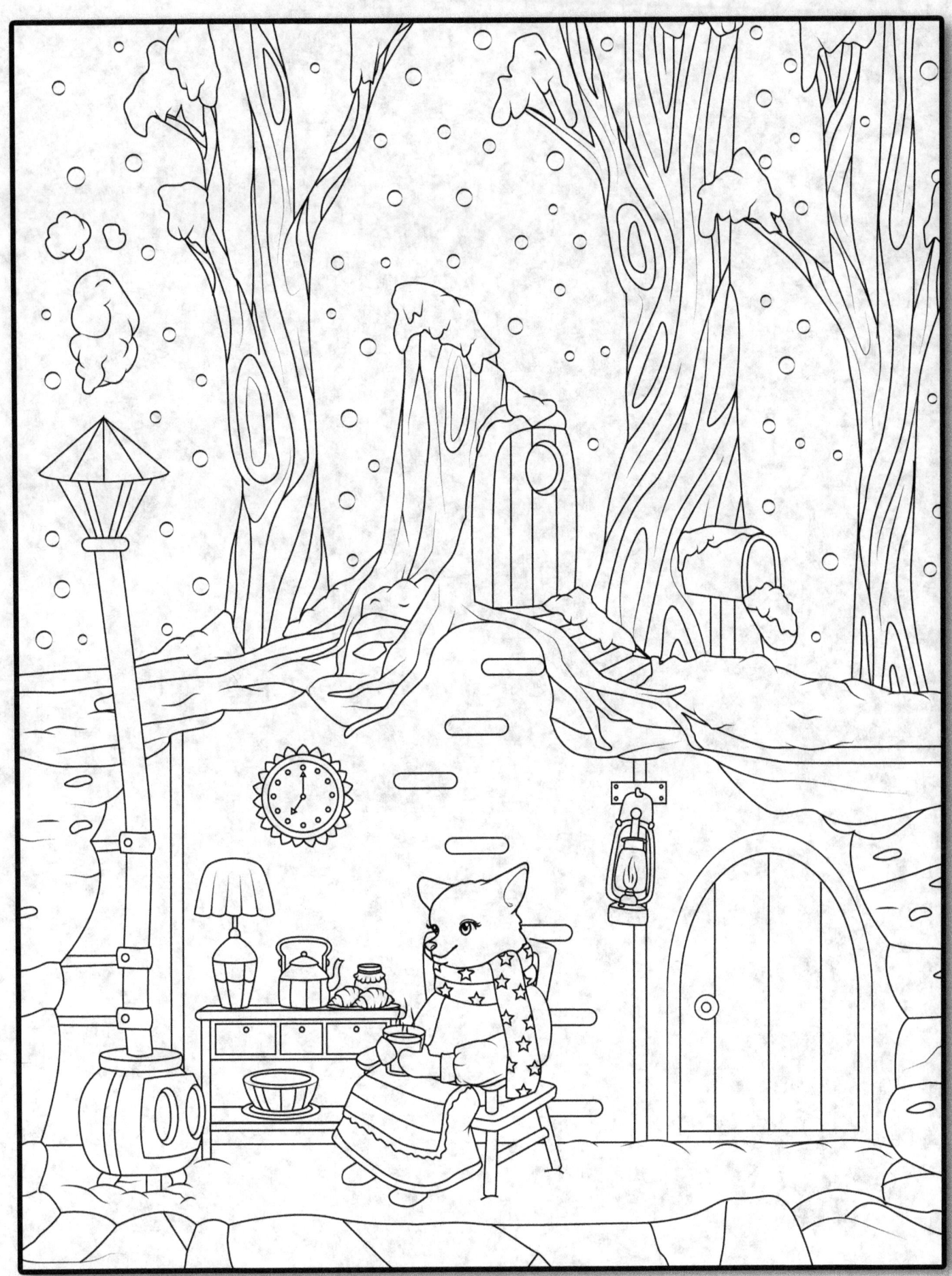

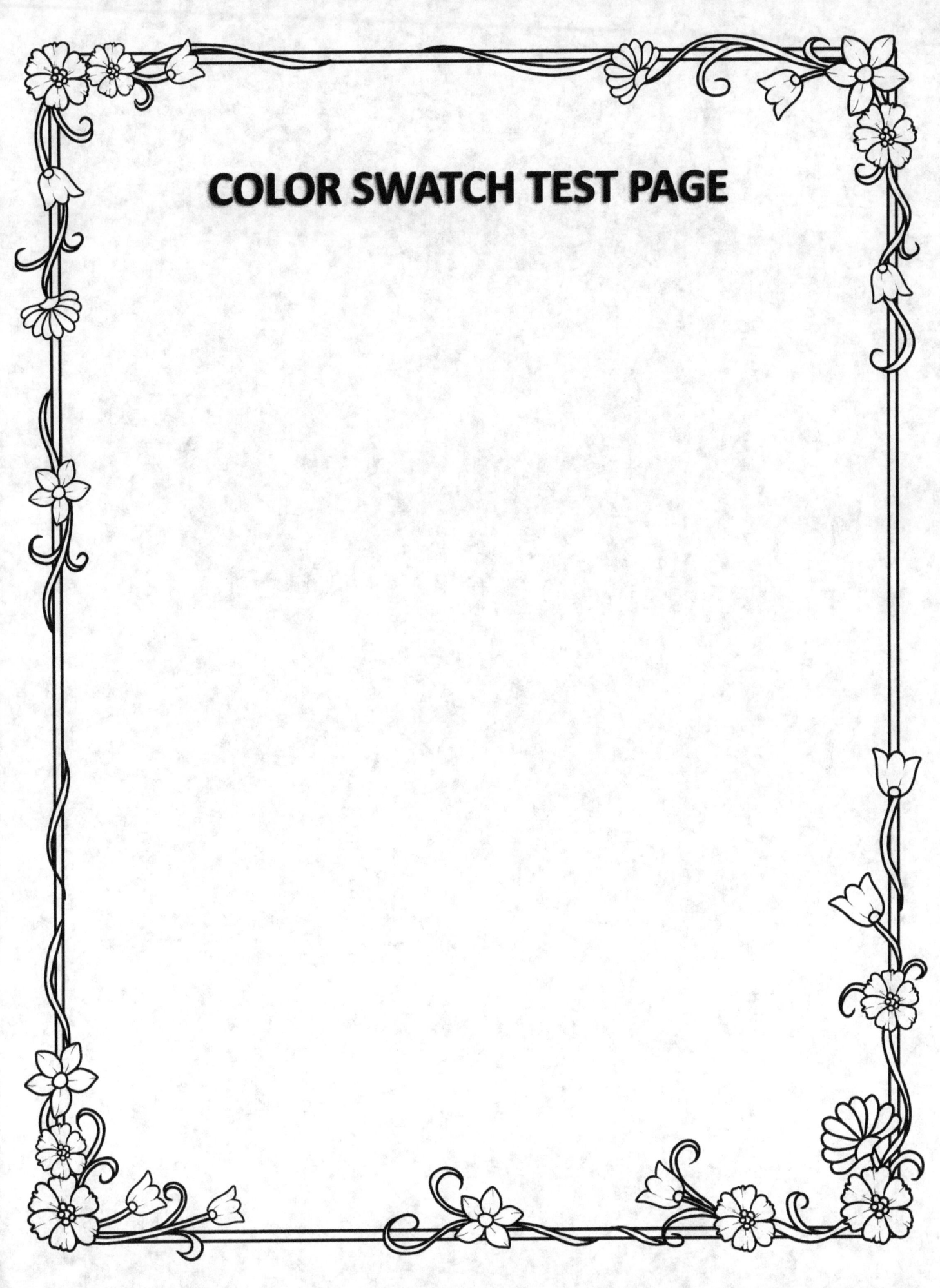

COLOR SWATCH TEST PAGE

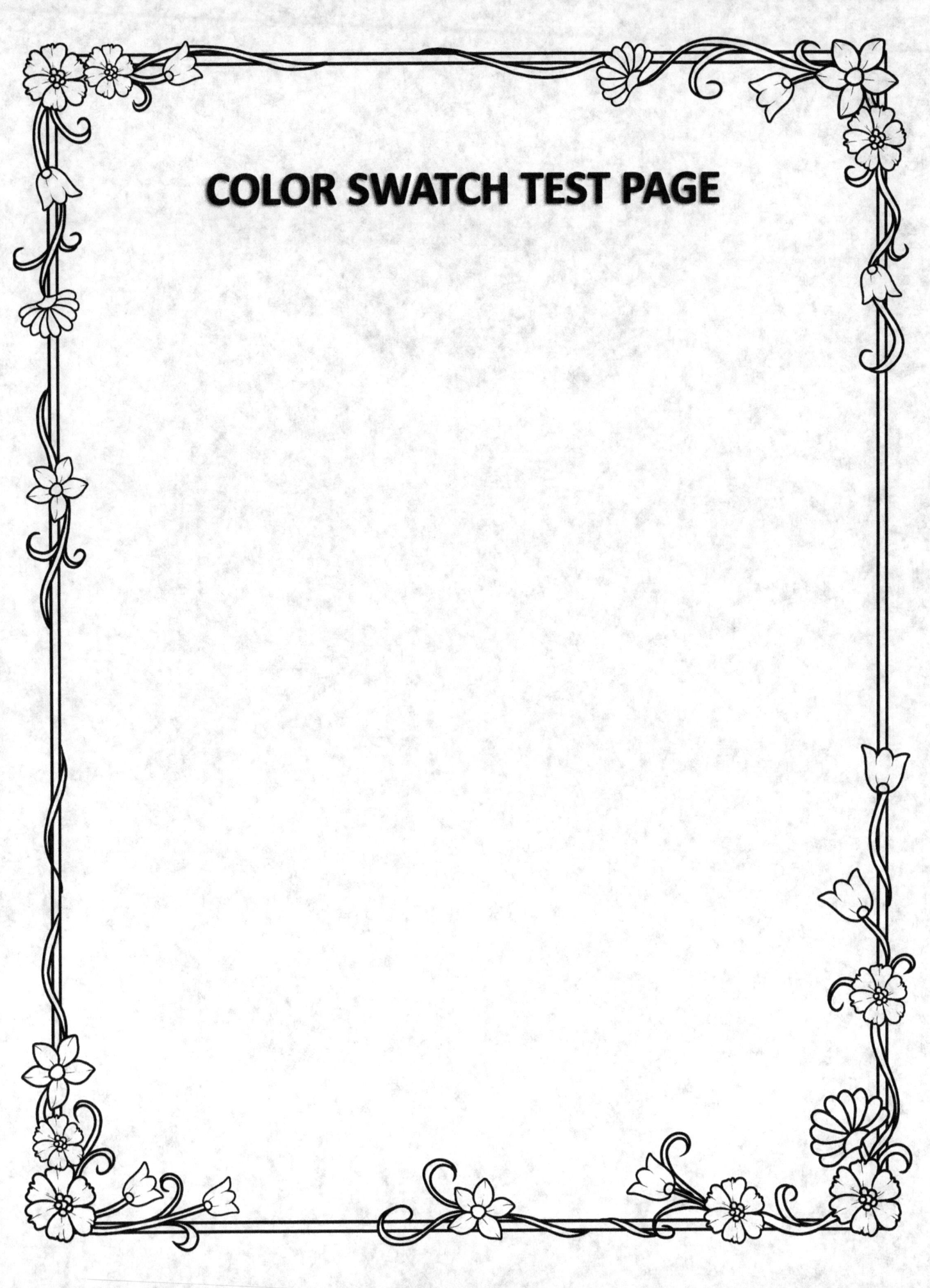

COLOR SWATCH TEST PAGE

COLOR SWATCH

BRAND: _____

PRODUCT NAME: _____

COLOR SWATCH

BRAND: _____

PRODUCT NAME: _____

COLOR SWATCH

BRAND: _____

PRODUCT NAME: _____

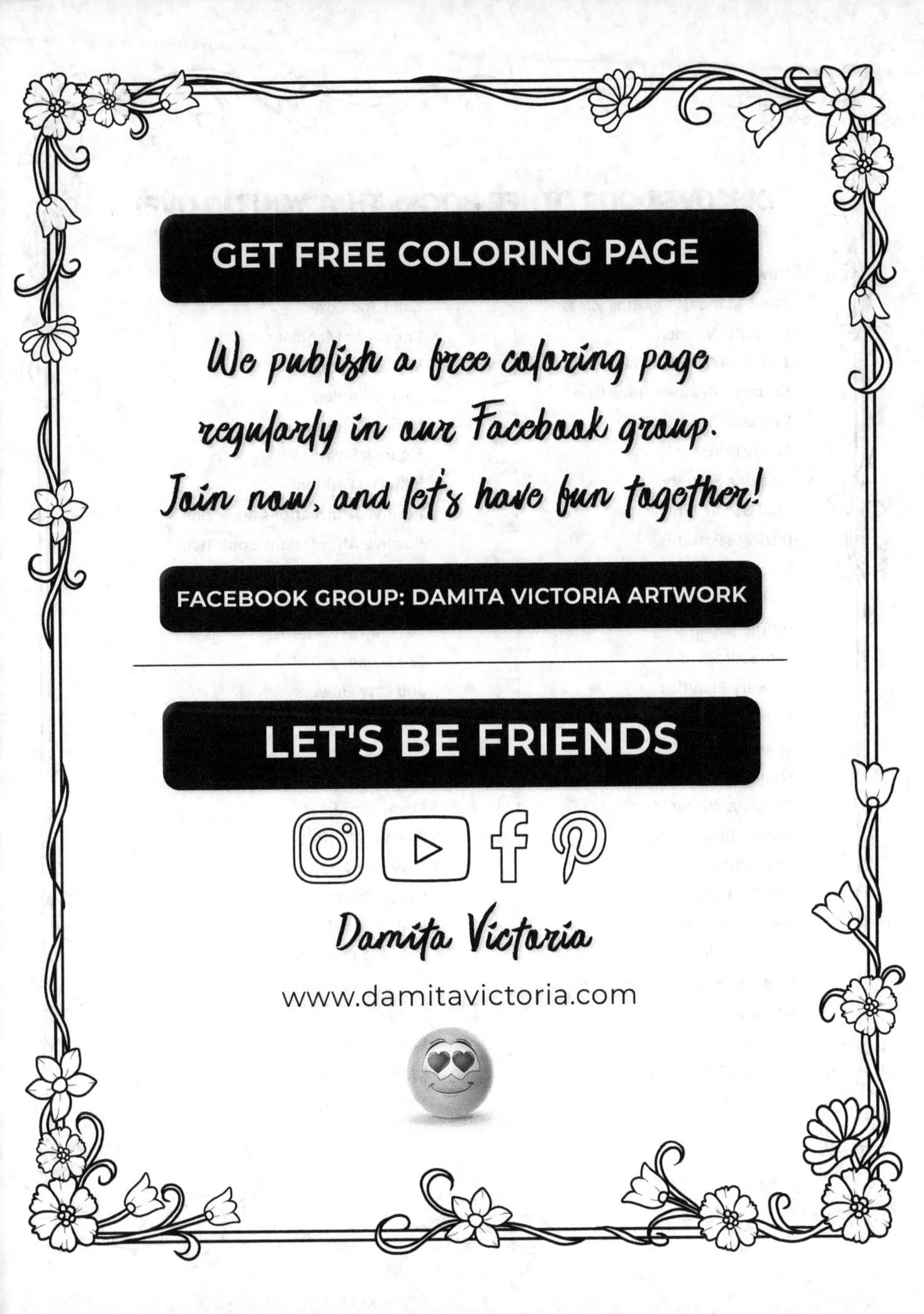

DISCOVER OUR OTHER BOOKS THAT YOU'LL LOVE!

- New-Fashioned Princesses ☐
- Adult Mandala Coloring Pages ☐
- Beautiful Women ☐
- 100 AMAZING Mandala ☐
- Fantastic Beauties Book One ☐
- Fantastic Beauties Two ☐
- Classy Princesa ☐
- Relaxing Scenery ☐
- Chill Out in Paris ☐
- Intricate Patterns ☐
- Summer on the Farm ☐
- Magical Wildland ☐
- By The Beach ☐
- Fantasticaland ☐
- Flowery Beauties ☐
- Happy Summer! ☐
- Charmer Beauty ☐
- Freaky Night ☐
- Relaxing Winter ☐
- Animal Reading Books ☐
- The Witches ☐
- 100 Coloring ☐
- Hello Autumn! ☐
- Mandala Flowers ☐
- Fantastic Beauties Book Three ☐
- Beautiful Patterns ☐
- Relaxing Mandalas ☐
- 100 Easy Mandalas ☐
- Pin-Up Models ☐

- Happy Season ☐
- Calm and Cozy ☐
- Christmas Mandalas ☐
- Winter Aesthetic ☐
- Lovely Garden ☐
- Whimsical Dreams ☐
- Flourish Swirls ☐
- Editorial Fashion ☐
- Positive Affirmations Book One ☐
- Positive Affirmations Book Two ☐
- Victorian Fashion ☐
- Love is Everwhere ☐
- Decorative Patterns ☐
- Zen Scenery ☐
- 100 Easy Flowers ☐
- Fantasialand ☐
- Floating Life ☐
- Magical Fairies ☐
- Floral Mandalas ☐
- Female Warriors ☐
- Cozy Interiors ☐
- Happy Easter ☐
- Hello Spring! ☐
- Amazing Patterns ☐
- Native American ☐
- Steampunk Art ☐
- Birds and Nature ☐
- Wolf Mandala ☐
- 100 Easy Coloring ☐

DISCOVER OUR OTHER BOOKS THAT YOU'LL LOVE!

- [ ] 100 Unique Patterns
- [ ] Mom's Daily Life
- [ ] Fairy Magicland
- [ ] Mermaids
- [ ] Summer Scenes
- [ ] Make Today Amazing
- [ ] Relaxing Patterns
- [ ] Global Beauties
- [ ] 100 Easy Autumn
- [ ] Harajuku Fashion
- [ ] Chibi Princesses
- [ ] 100 Mandalas
- [ ] Fantasy World
- [ ] Autumn Patterns
- [ ] Goddesses and Warriors
- [ ] Autumn Scenes
- [ ] 50 Autumn Mandalas
- [ ] Victorian Chibi
- [ ] World of Animals
- [ ] Magical Unicorn
- [ ] Haunted House
- [ ] Vampires
- [ ] Freaks Beauties
- [ ] Winter Wonderland
- [ ] Jolly Winter
- [ ] 100 Easy Winter
- [ ] Advent Calendar
- [ ] Shape and Beauty
- [ ] Christmas

- [ ] Dreamcatchers
- [ ] 100 Lovely Swirls
- [ ] Mystical Patterns
- [ ] Angels
- [ ] Cute Animals
- [ ] The Dragon Queen
- [ ] Rustic Cabins
- [ ] 100 Easy Spring
- [ ] Chill & Relax
- [ ] Adorable Cuties
- [ ] Farm Scenes
- [ ] 100 Easy Summer
- [ ] Quirky Vintage
- [ ] Autumn Cuties
- [ ] 100 Super Easy
- [ ] Cozy Landscape
- [ ] Worlds of Music
- [ ] 100 Relaxing Flowers
- [ ] 100 Gardens & Flowers
- [ ] Wondrousland
- [ ] Terrarium Life
- [ ] Male Portraits
- [ ] Fantastical Room
- [ ] Counting to Christmas
- [ ] Dreamer Fantasy
- [ ] Whimsical Patterns
- [ ] Retro Portraits
- [ ] Old Western
- [ ] Winter Burrow

WRITE AMAZON REVIEWS

WE'D LOVE YOUR FEEDBACK...

We'd love to know how everything worked out for you, don't be a stranger! Join the conversation and share your feedback with us.

Find this book on Amazon, scroll to the customer reviews, and please let us know your thoughts and comments.

We'd love to hear your feedback so we can continue to improve our service to you.

GET FREE BOOK

www.damitavictoria.com

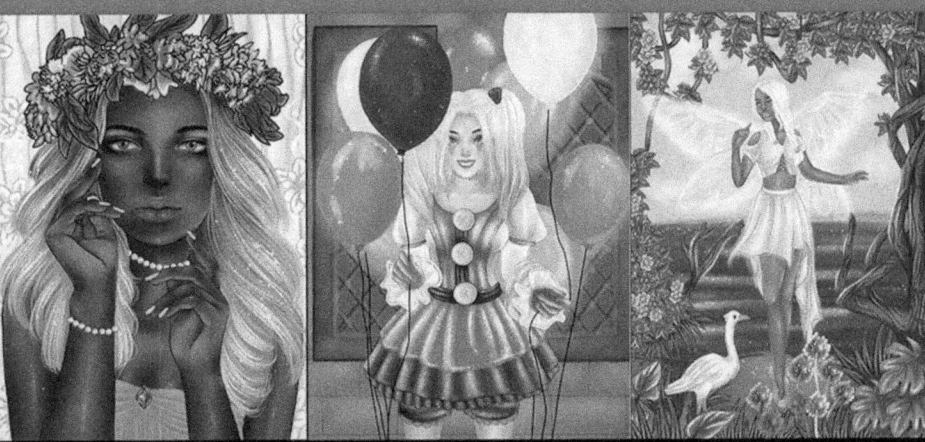

100 COLORING
RELAXATION COLORING BOOKS FOR ADULTS WITH 100 IMAGES FROM RANDOM THEMES

Damita Victoria

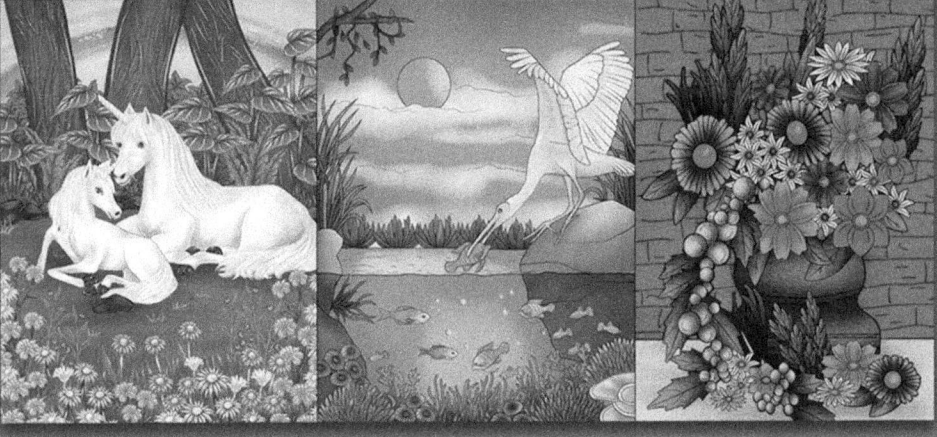

Subcribe to our news letter and get the digital version of "100 Coloring Book" for free.

To Download The Book Visit
www.damitavictoria.com/free-coloring-page

www.ingramcontent.com/pod-product-compliance
Lightning Source LLC
Chambersburg PA
CBHW080508220526
45465CB00006B/2418